KS2 English
Comprehension

Teacher Book One — Years 3-6

This Teacher Book accompanies the first set of CGP's
Targeted Comprehension Question Books for Years 3-6.

It includes answers to every question, essential
background information for each text, suggestions for
extension activities, pupil progress charts... and more!

It's ideal for helping you plan and organise your
Guided Reading sessions throughout Key Stage Two.

Contents

Key Stage Two Reading Comprehension...1

The Targeted Question Books...2

The Teacher Book...3

Planning and Delivery..4

Marking and Monitoring Progress..5

Genre Charts...6

Cross-Curricular Subject Charts..10

Year 3

Harriet's Hare by Dick King-Smith 14

Building Stonehenge by Martin Oliver 15

Nature Trail by Benjamin Zephaniah..16

Bill's New Frock by Anne Fine...17

Let's Get Growing! by Chris Collins and Lia Leendertz 18

Daddy Fell into the Pond by Alfred Noyes 19

The Demon Headmaster by Gillian Cross 20

Robotic Baby Penguin from The Independent 21

High Adventure by Sir Edmund Hillary 22

An Interview with Rebecca Adlington...23

My Name is Mina by David Almond..24

Poems about Crocodiles by Lewis Carroll and Christine F. Fletcher 25

The Secret History of Tom Trueheart by Ian Beck..26

Jellyfish in the UK from The Independent..27

Carrie's War by Nina Bawden 28

Year 4

Choosing a Bike from www.nhs.uk 29

The Tale of Custard the Dragon by Ogden Nash...30

Aesop's Fables by Aesop...31

An Interview with Jacqueline Wilson 32

Harry Drinkwater's Diary 33

Hamish and the Worldstoppers by Danny Wallace 34

BBC Women's Footballer of the Year from Prolific North 35

The Real Princess by Hans Christian Andersen 36

Chinese New Year by Alex Fairer 37

The Girl Who Walked On Air by Emma Carroll 38

Reign of the Sea Dragons by Sneed Collard 39

Peter Pan by J.M. Barrie 40

Bletchley Park Codebreakers from The Telegraph 41

Poems about Witches by Percy H. Ilott and Alexander Resnikoff.........42

Swim, Bike, Run: Our Triathlon Story by Alistair and Jonathan Brownlee 43

Year 5

The Word Party by Richard Edwards 44

An Astronaut's Guide to Life on Earth by Chris Hadfield 45

Why Recycle? from www.thinkcans.net...................................46

Tales of King Arthur by Felicity Brooks 47

The Great Fire of London by George Szirtes...........................48

The Iron Man by Ted Hughes 49

Pompeii by Catherine Heygate 50

From a Railway Carriage by Robert Louis Stevenson....................51

Tracking Basking Sharks from The Independent 52

A Letter from E.B. White 53

Poems about Knights by Hugh Chesterman and Sir Walter Scott..........54

The Wind in the Willows (musical) by Stephen Kingsbury and Ben Sleep.......55

Hiding Out by Elizabeth Laird..56

Wolves in the UK from The Independent 57

The Wolves of Willoughby Chase by Joan Aiken........................58

Year 6

An Interview with Nixie Labs..59

Holes by Louis Sachar..60

Born on a Blue Day by Daniel Tammet..61

Hostages to Handheld Devices from The Independent................................62

Cider With Rosie by Laurie Lee..63

Olympic Torch Relay, Day 52 from The Guardian................................64

Poems about Seasons by Adrian Henri and John Updike................................65

A Letter from C.S. Lewis..66

The Lord of the Rings by J.R.R. Tolkien..67

Queen Victoria's Diary..68

If— by Rudyard Kipling..69

Theseus's Adventures by H.A. Guerber..70

I Can Jump Puddles by Alan Marshall..71

White Fang by Jack London..72

Macbeth by William Shakespeare..73

Pupil Progress Charts..74

When using the Extra Activities in this product, please take the safety of the participants into consideration at all times, and ensure that children are supervised when researching material for this product online. Teachers should also take into account pupils' personal circumstances when dealing with topics of a sensitive nature.

Published by CGP

Editors: Alex Fairer, Rachel Grocott, Ceara Hayden, Catherine Heygate
Consultants: Samantha Bensted, Amanda MacNaughton, Maxine Petrie
Proofreaders: Janet Berkeley, Alison Griffin, Lucy Loveluck, Heather McClelland, Holly Poynton, Glenn Rogers

With thanks to Laura Jakubowski for the copyright research.

ISBN: 978 1 78294 470 6
Printed by Elanders Ltd, Newcastle upon Tyne.
Images on pages 46 and 56 from Corel®
Illustrations on pages 15, 16, 18, 21, 25, 28, 29, 39, 42, 51, 54, 55, 57, 63, 66, 68, 70, 73 © clipart.com

Key Stage Two Reading Comprehension

In this introduction, you'll find everything you need to help you get the most out of CGP's Key Stage Two Targeted Comprehension range.

Reading comprehension is a key part of the National Curriculum

The English Programme of Study for the Key Stage Two National Curriculum requires pupils to explore a wide variety of fiction and non-fiction texts. Pupils are expected to:

- develop increasingly advanced reading comprehension skills;

- expand their vocabulary;

- improve the accuracy and fluency with which they read;

- develop their ability to understand and make inferences about complex and challenging texts.

CGP's Key Stage Two Targeted Comprehension range

- CGP's Key Stage Two Targeted Comprehension range is designed to support the development and assessment of pupils' reading comprehension skills throughout years 3 to 6. It is ideal for use in Guided Reading sessions.

- The range is packed full of high-quality texts, from a variety of authors and sources, that will instil in pupils a love of reading and encourage them to read more widely and deeply.

- It consists of four Targeted Question Books (see page 2 for more information)...

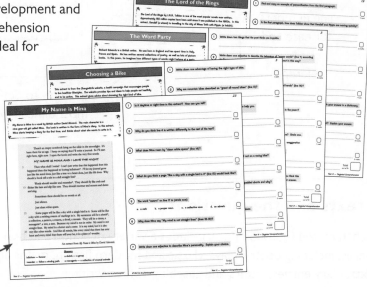

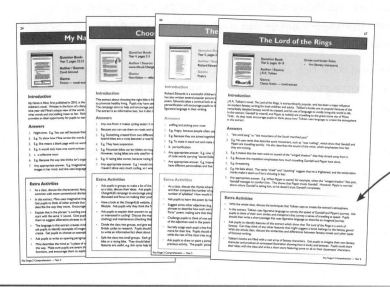

- ...and an accompanying Teacher Book. The range can be used in Guided Reading sessions, or as the foundation for a variety of other literacy lessons and activities.

- Many of the Extra Activities in the Teacher Book have been designed to support teaching across the whole Key Stage Two curriculum — see pages 3 and 4 for how to incorporate the texts into your scheme of work.

The Targeted Question Books

What are the Targeted Question Books?

The Key Stage Two Targeted Comprehension range includes four Targeted Question Books — one each for years 3, 4, 5 and 6. Each book contains fifteen engaging texts, accompanied by challenging and stimulating questions.

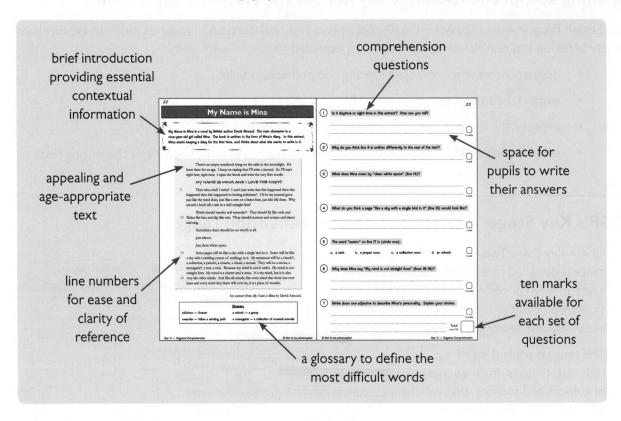

brief introduction providing essential contextual information

comprehension questions

appealing and age-appropriate text

space for pupils to write their answers

line numbers for ease and clarity of reference

ten marks available for each set of questions

a glossary to define the most difficult words

The texts and the questions

- Each Targeted Question Book includes a variety of fiction and non-fiction texts, drawn from different genres, including poetry, plays, classic and modern fiction, myths and legends, news articles, reference texts, diary entries, letters and autobiographical writing.

- The texts have been carefully chosen to capture the interest of Key Stage Two pupils and promote enjoyment of reading. They have been taken from age-appropriate sources that will inspire many pupils to read the rest of the text independently.

- The texts deal with a wide variety of topics, and their rich and varied subject matter will appeal to girls and boys alike. As well as building on pupils' existing knowledge, they will introduce pupils to new concepts and ideas that will often form the basis for thought-provoking discussions.

- Each text is followed by a set of comprehension questions. These questions test a range of reading comprehension skills: retrieving facts; summarising information; making inferences; defining words in context; identifying literary and presentational techniques; and explaining the effect of these techniques on the reader. Some questions require pupils to draw on their own opinions and experiences, encouraging them to relate to the text on a personal level.

The Teacher Book

What is the Teacher Book?

This Teacher Book will help you to use the texts in the Targeted Question Books to their full potential, incorporating texts from all four books into your planning. It provides an introduction to each text, full answers to the questions in the Targeted Question Books and suggestions for literacy-based and cross-curricular Extra Activities. Used together, the questions and Extra Activities will help pupils engage with and show they have understood the texts, as well as enabling you to assess and monitor the development of their comprehension skills.

introduction providing useful background information

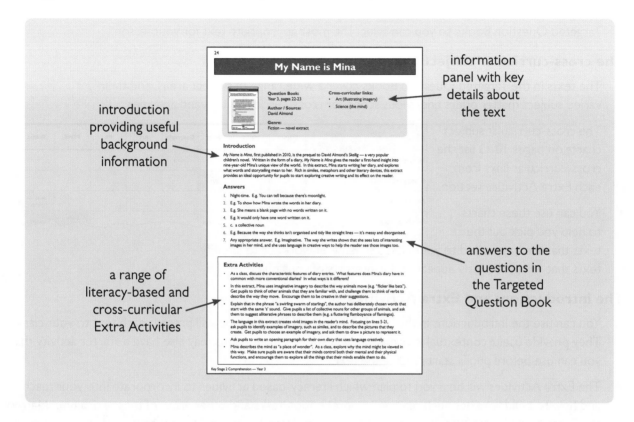

information panel with key details about the text

answers to the questions in the Targeted Question Book

a range of literacy-based and cross-curricular Extra Activities

Use the Teacher Book alongside the Targeted Question Books

- To help you find the information you need quickly and easily, the Teacher Book pages are colour-coded to match the colour of the Question Books — purple for Year 3, green for Year 4, orange for Year 5 and turquoise for Year 6.

- The information panel at the top of each page provides the key details about each text. It includes the Targeted Question Book page reference, author or source, genre and cross-curricular links.

- The concise introductions give you all the information you need to present each text to your class, highlighting important facts and concepts that pupils should be aware of before they start reading.

- The answer section for each text contains answers for fact-retrieval questions, and appropriate suggestions and example answers for more complex questions. See page 5 for more about the answers.

- A range of stimulating Extra Activities is provided. These extension activities are all linked to the text and can be used to enhance pupils' understanding of the text, topic and genre. See page 4 for more information about the cross-curricular links in the Extra Activities.

Planning and Delivery

Planning your lessons...

The texts in the Targeted Question Books can be used in any order. The Teacher Book has several useful features that will help you select which texts to use and plan how to incorporate them into your teaching.

The genre charts

- The English National Curriculum requires Key Stage Two pupils to read and discuss a wide range of texts.

- The genre charts on pages 6-9 of this book allow you to easily identify the genre(s) of each text in the Targeted Question Books so you can select the most appropriate text for your lesson.

The cross-curricular subject charts

- The texts in the Targeted Question Books cover a wide range of subject areas, and their varied subject matter offers enormous scope for cross-curricular links and activities.

- The cross-curricular subject charts on pages 10-13 list the cross-curricular links from each Extra Activities section.

	Science	Maths	History	Geography	Art	PE	PSHE	Drama	D&T
Harriet's Hare	hares; crop circles			valleys					
Building Stonehenge			prehistory						
Nature Trail	identifying organisms							acting out verses	
Bill's New Frock							gender	playscript	

- You can use these charts to help you pick out the texts that are best-suited to your class's scheme of work, or to identify texts that will particularly appeal to the interests of your pupils.

The introductions and Extra Activities

- You can use the introductions in the Teacher Book to plan how you will present each text to your class. They provide useful contextual information, and some introductions may also have a starter activity that you can use before pupils start reading the text.

- The Extra Activities will help you to plan which literacy-based activities to incorporate into your teaching and how to build links between reading comprehension tasks and other areas of the curriculum. Many of the Extra Activities are transferable and could also be used alongside different texts and as a foundation for teaching across the whole Key Stage Two curriculum.

Using the texts...

Once you've finished planning, follow these tips to help pupils get to grips with the texts.

Encourage pupils to read carefully

- The introduction to each text in the Targeted Question Books provides useful information about the text and its author or the context in which it was written. This background information is important for pupils' understanding of the text, and pupils should always read it before moving on to the text itself.

- Get pupils to read the introduction and text thoroughly before tackling the questions. Once they are familiar with the content, ask them to read the questions and revisit the text to pick out the key details they need to answer the questions.

- A glossary is provided with some texts, defining the most challenging words. However, pupils should be encouraged to look up any other unfamiliar words in a dictionary and check answers to vocabulary-based questions themselves. Note that as the range contains a variety of genres and authors, some texts use American English spellings. Where appropriate, you may wish to explain this difference to pupils.

- Once pupils have completed the questions, move on to the Extra Activities that you have selected — many of these build on pupils' answers to questions in the Targeted Question Books.

Marking and Monitoring Progress

The Key Stage Two Targeted Comprehension range includes helpful tools to enable you to check how well your class has understood each text and how their comprehension skills are progressing.

There are ten marks available for each set of questions

Because the questions for each text are marked out of ten, you can easily compare a pupil's performance over the various texts, and see which genres pupils need more practice with. To help you to mark pupils' answers, the Teacher Book provides answers to all of the questions from all four of the Targeted Question Books.

Use your own judgement

- The answers provided in the Teacher Book are intended as a guide only, and you will need to use your own judgement when marking pupils' responses.

- Answers preceded by "E.g." require pupils to offer their own interpretation of the information contained in the text. There is often no 'correct answer', but pupils' answers should be based on the text and go into a similar amount of detail as the sample answer.

- Answers marked "Any appropriate answer" require pupils to offer their own opinions. Again, there is no 'correct answer', and the answers given in the Teacher Book are just suggestions. However, pupils should show a clear understanding of the question and give reasons to support their answer.

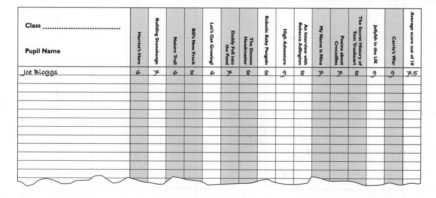

Monitoring pupil progress

- Use the four progress charts starting on page 74 to help you keep track of pupils' progress — there is a chart for each year group.

- The progress charts are colour-coded so you can easily distinguish between fiction and non-fiction texts and check which genres your class needs more practice with.

Your turn...

Each Targeted Question Book ends with a 'your turn' activity. See how well pupils' comprehension skills have developed by challenging them to write their own text and construct a series of questions about it. The challenge of writing questions further develops pupils' literacy skills and gives them a new perspective on text comprehension. This activity also provides an opportunity for group or partner work — pupils can swap the texts and questions they have written and attempt to answer each other's questions.

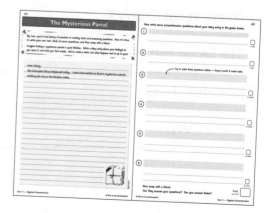

Genre Chart — Year 3

	Non-fiction	Fiction	Classic fiction	Autobiography / Memoir	News article	Playscript	Poetry	Classic poetry	Diary	Letter	Myth / Legend
Harriet's Hare		✓									
Building Stonehenge	✓										
Nature Trail							✓				
Bill's New Frock		✓									
Let's Get Growing!	✓										
Daddy Fell into the Pond								✓			
The Demon Headmaster		✓									
Robotic Baby Penguin					✓						
High Adventure				✓							
An Interview with Rebecca Adlington	✓										
My Name is Mina		✓							✓		
Poems about Crocodiles							✓				
The Secret History of Tom Trueheart		✓									
Jellyfish in the UK					✓						
Carrie's War		✓									

Genre Chart — Year 4

	Non-fiction	Fiction	Classic fiction	Autobiography / Memoir	News article	Playscript	Poetry	Classic poetry	Diary	Letter	Myth / Legend
Choosing a Bike	✓										
The Tale of Custard the Dragon								✓			
Aesop's Fables		✓									
An Interview with Jacqueline Wilson	✓										
Harry Drinkwater's Diary									✓		
Hamish and the Worldstoppers		✓									
BBC Women's Footballer of the Year					✓						
The Real Princess			✓								
Chinese New Year	✓										
The Girl Who Walked On Air		✓									
Reign of the Sea Dragons	✓										
Peter Pan			✓								
Bletchley Park Codebreakers					✓						
Poems about Witches							✓				
Swim, Bike, Run: Our Triathlon Story				✓							

Genre Chart — Year 5

	Non-fiction	Fiction	Classic fiction	Autobiography / Memoir	News article	Playscript	Poetry	Classic poetry	Diary	Letter	Myth / Legend
The Word Party							✓				
An Astronaut's Guide to Life on Earth				✓							
Why Recycle?	✓										
Tales of King Arthur		✓									✓
The Great Fire of London							✓				
The Iron Man		✓									
Pompeii	✓										
From a Railway Carriage								✓			
Tracking Basking Sharks					✓						
A Letter from E.B. White										✓	
Poems about Knights								✓			
The Wind in the Willows (musical)		✓				✓					
Hiding Out		✓									
Wolves in the UK					✓						
The Wolves of Willoughby Chase			✓								

Genre Chart — Year 6

	Non-fiction	Fiction	Classic fiction	Autobiography / Memoir	News article	Playscript	Poetry	Classic poetry	Diary	Letter	Myth / Legend
An Interview with Nixie Labs	✓										
Holes		✓									
Born on a Blue Day				✓							
Hostages to Handheld Devices					✓						
Cider With Rosie			✓	✓							
Olympic Torch Relay, Day 52					✓						
Poems about Seasons							✓				
A Letter from C.S. Lewis										✓	
The Lord of the Rings			✓								
Queen Victoria's Diary									✓		
If—								✓			
Theseus's Adventures											✓
I Can Jump Puddles				✓							
White Fang			✓								
Macbeth			✓			✓					

Cross-Curricular Subject Chart — Year 3

	Science	Maths	History	Geography	Art	PE	PSHE	Drama	D&T
Harriet's Hare	hares; crop circles			valleys					
Building Stonehenge			prehistory						
Nature Trail	identifying organisms							acting out verses	
Bill's New Frock							gender inequality	playscript	
Let's Get Growing!	bees and pollination						growing your own food		designing a garden
Daddy Fell into the Pond								performance	
The Demon Headmaster		multiplication		Europe					
Robotic Baby Penguin	penguins; robots	ordering numbers			illustrating a text				designing a robot
High Adventure				tourism			setting goals		
An Interview with Rebecca Adlington	nutrition								
My Name is Mina	the mind				illustrating imagery				
Poems about Crocodiles	Nile crocodiles								
The Secret History of Tom Trueheart					cartoon strip		being different		
Jellyfish in the UK	grouping animals				making a collage				
Carrie's War			evacuation				family relationships		

Cross-Curricular Subject Chart — Year 4

	Science	Maths	History	Geography	Art	PE	PSHE	Drama	D&T
Choosing a Bike							healthy lifestyle; bike safety		bike design
The Tale of Custard the Dragon							courage; friendship	performance	
Aesop's Fables			life of Aesop				relating to others		
An Interview with Jacqueline Wilson	dreams				book cover		personal achievements		
Harry Drinkwater's Diary			World War One; sources		war paintings				
Hamish and the Worldstoppers	time zones							performance	
BBC Women's Footballer of the Year		statistics		international football		football tournament	gender inequality		
The Real Princess					storyboards			role-play	
Chinese New Year		multiples			illustrating a text		different cultures		
The Girl Who Walked On Air	gravity	multiplication and division	Victorian circus				animal welfare		
Reign of the Sea Dragons	adaptation; food webs	conversion; scale							
Peter Pan							growing up	playscript	
Bletchley Park Codebreakers		cyphers; sequences	World War Two						
Poems about Witches			superstitions		illustration				
Swim, Bike, Run: Our Triathlon Story				UK towns and cities			role models		

Cross-Curricular Subject Chart — Year 5

	Science	Maths	History	Geography	Art	PE	PSHE	Drama	D&T
The Word Party					illustrating imagery			mime	
An Astronaut's Guide to Life on Earth	the solar system						ambitions		building a sundial
Why Recycle?	pollution	statistics					recycling		
Tales of King Arthur			reliability of sources						
The Great Fire of London			the Great Fire of London	using maps					
The Iron Man	properties of materials	nets							
Pompeii			the Roman Empire	volcanoes	mosaics				
From a Railway Carriage		timetables	Victorian railways						
Tracking Basking Sharks	marine organisms				drawing activity				
A Letter from E.B. White	spiders								
Poems about Knights					designing shields				
The Wind in the Willows (musical)							crime and the law	role-play	
Hiding Out			prehistoric Europe		cave paintings				
Wolves in the UK	wolves								
The Wolves of Willoughby Chase					cartoon strip			scriptwriting	

Cross-Curricular Subject Chart — Year 6

	Science	Maths	History	Geography	Art	PE	PSHE	Drama	D&T
An Interview with Nixie Labs	technological innovation		famous inventors						testing prototypes
Holes				deserts			juvenile prison	role-play	
Born on a Blue Day		prime numbers			numerical representation		autism spectrum		
Hostages to Handheld Devices	benefits of exercise	statistics				sport and technology			
Cider With Rosie			change over time	the British landscape					
Olympic Torch Relay, Day 52			Ancient Greece	world cities			disability and accessibility		
Poems about Seasons				comparing climates					
A Letter from C.S. Lewis					illustrating a text				
The Lord of the Rings					fantasy characters				
Queen Victoria's Diary			sources						
If—							personal development		
Theseus's Adventures			Ancient Greece				democracy		
I Can Jump Puddles				Australia; tourism			disability		
White Fang	adaptation and evolution			Yukon Territory					
Macbeth					cartoon strip		ambition	performance	

Harriet's Hare

Question Book:
Year 3, pages 2-3

Author / Source:
Dick King-Smith

Genre:
Fiction — novel extract

Cross-curricular links:

• Geography (valleys)

• Science (hares; crop circles)

Introduction

Dick King-Smith was an extremely prolific and popular children's author, and some pupils may already be familiar with his books. Inspired by his childhood love of animals and the years he spent as a farmer, many of his books are centred on animals. *Harriet's Hare* is unique as it also contains an element of science fiction — the hare of the title is an alien. This alien has taken on the form of a talking hare, who is discovered by 8-year-old Harriet in her father's wheatfield, leading to their firm friendship. Note that in this extract, "corn" refers to cereal plants in general, rather than a specific crop.

Answers

1. E.g. The green field is a field of grass; the gold field is a field of wheat.

2. E.g. The cows would usually be waiting near the gate of their field for Harriet's father to take them to be milked, but instead, they're running and jumping around in the field.

3. E.g. The field is completely covered by wheat, so it looks as though a golden blanket has been spread over it. It seems like there's a hole in the blanket because there's a circle of flattened corn in a corner of the field.

4. E.g. She wants to find out what has made the circle in the field of corn.

5. E.g. It means that the hillside is covered in drops of water.

6. E.g. To show that Harriet is puzzled and curious about what has happened.

7. E.g. She is surprised because wild animals don't usually get so close to humans, and then she is amazed because animals can't talk, but the hare talks to her.

Extra Activities

• Ask the pupils to imagine that they are the author of *Harriet's Hare*. Get them to continue writing the story, which should focus on Harriet's reaction to the talking hare.

• Discuss the author's use of descriptive language to introduce the agricultural setting and how the extract builds an atmosphere of intrigue and mystery. Get the pupils to write their own short story, paying particular attention to the setting and creating an atmosphere of mystery.

• To help pupils understand the setting of *Harriet's Hare*, explain what a valley is using pictures from books or the Internet. Ask pupils to draw what they imagine the setting of the extract to look like.

• Make sure the class understands what a hare is by exploring the differences between a hare and a rabbit. Get pupils to make a list of their similarities and differences.

• Explain that the hare in the book is an alien which has taken on the form of an animal. Explain that, although evidence suggests crop circles are man-made, some people believe they are made by aliens. Show pupils pictures of crop circles and initiate a discussion about what could have made them.

Building Stonehenge

Question Book:
Year 3, pages 4-5

Author / Source:
Martin Oliver

Genre:
Non-fiction — reference text

Cross-curricular links:
* History (prehistory)

Introduction

Stonehenge's construction began in roughly 3100 BC in Wiltshire. Although the reason why Stonehenge was built remains a mystery, archaeologists believe that it was made to celebrate the changing seasons or to worship the sun. This extract, taken from a book which aims to help children understand and enjoy British history, explains the three different phases in the construction of Stonehenge.

If some children in the class have visited Stonehenge, encourage them to tell the others what it was like. The text refers to 'BC' a number of times, so explain the significance of this while reading the text.

Answers

1. E.g. Because some of them are still standing today.

2. E.g. To celebrate the changing seasons and to worship the sun.

3. a. They weighed up to 4 tonnes. d. They formed another two circles.

4. E.g. A ring of stones which were laid on top.

5. E.g. Its subheadings split up the information so that each phase of Stonehenge's construction is separated. This makes each different phase clearer to the reader.

6. Any appropriate answer. E.g. Yes, I would like to visit Stonehenge because it sounds very interesting and you don't usually get the chance to see something made in prehistoric times.

Extra Activities

* Invite pupils to imagine they were present at the construction of Stonehenge or that they went to visit it once completed. Ask them to write a short diary entry about their experiences and how they felt.

* Ask pupils to design a leaflet informing people about Stonehenge. They should focus on presenting the most important information from the extract in a clear and easy-to-understand way.

* Introduce the class to the concept of prehistory — the period of time before the appearance of written records. Ask pupils why they think this creates challenges if we want to find out about Stonehenge.

* Using a map, show pupils the distance between Stonehenge and the Preseli Hills in Wales, where some of the stones were brought from. Ask the class why they think transporting the stones would have been difficult for early Britons. Get them to discuss the methods of transportation they think were used.

Nature Trail

Question Book:
Year 3, pages 6-7

Author / Source:
Benjamin Zephaniah

Genre:
Poetry

Cross-curricular links:
*   Drama (acting out verses)

*   Science (identifying organisms)

Introduction

Benjamin Zephaniah, a British poet, has been inspired by his Jamaican heritage to create musical and rhythmic poetry. Zephaniah is a performance poet who enjoys touring all over the world to perform his poems to live audiences and for television audiences. The poetry he has created for children is popular for its strong rhythm and humour while still conveying important messages. *Nature Trail* has a sing-song rhythm and describes the animals Zephaniah observes in his garden, finishing with a reflection on the importance of gardens and nature in people's lives.

Answers

1. underneath a log

2. E.g. Because snails move slowly.

3. Birds and cats. E.g. Some cats kill birds, so birds will avoid the garden when cats are there, but cats will go into the garden when birds are there.

4. a fox

5. E.g. steal; pinch; take

6. E.g. Animals are always searching for food, and plants are always growing.

7. E.g. There are always things going on in gardens that you can watch, and all this activity means you will never be alone.

Extra Activities

*   Read the poem out loud with the class. Ask them to think about the rhythm of the poem and to look out for pairs of rhyming words. It may help to introduce pupils to half-rhymes, such as "time" and "mine" in lines 14 and 16.

*   Split the class into groups and assign a verse to each group. Ask each group to come up with actions for their verse which they should then perform to the class as they read their verse aloud.

*   Ask pupils to think of other plants and animals that might be found in a garden. As a class, write your own verse for the poem, including some of the plants and animals pupils suggested. Write the verse in the same style as Zephaniah, following the same rhythm and rhyme scheme.

*   Get pupils to write a short story set in Zephaniah's garden. They should develop the characters of some of the animals in the poem, and think about how they might interact with each other.

*   Take the class outside to see what wildlife they can observe. How many different plants can they see? Can they see any insects, birds or other animals? Ask pupils to make sketches of the plants and animals they see, and to take note of key features such as colour, markings, size and where they were found. Once back inside, pupils should do some research to try and identify the plants and animals they observed.

Bill's New Frock

Question Book:
Year 3, pages 8-9

Author / Source:
Anne Fine

Genre:
Fiction — novel extract

Cross-curricular links:
- PSHE (gender inequality)
- Drama (playscript)

Introduction

Bill's New Frock centres on Bill, a boy who wakes up one morning to find that he has turned into a girl. In the course of his day living as a girl, Bill is frustrated to discover the many ways in which girls are treated differently to boys. Anne Fine wrote *Bill's New Frock* following research she conducted in schools, which showed that teachers often treat boys and girls differently (e.g. not expecting girls to be interested in adventure books). Through Bill's character, Fine aims to make children aware of gender inequality, and to remind teachers that all children should be treated the same, regardless of their gender.

Answers

1. E.g. confused; bewildered; mystified

2. E.g. She thinks girls should wear pretty dresses and like the colour pink.

3. Any appropriate answer. E.g. His parents were both in a hurry, so he didn't really get a chance to argue with them. He might also have been too surprised and confused to think about arguing.

4. E.g. She doesn't behave any differently towards Bill, unlike his parents, who are treating him as if he's a girl.

5. E.g. Bad things happen in nightmares, and Bill feels that something bad might happen to him when he walks past Mean Malcolm.

6. Any appropriate answer. E.g. They might expect Bill to play with the girls rather than the boys, and to like things like dolls and dresses.

Extra Activities

- With the whole class, discuss pupils' answers to question 6 in the Question Book. Do pupils think that boys and girls are treated differently? Do they think it's fair for boys and girls to be treated differently? Ask pupils to identify stereotypes relating to boys and girls. As a class, explore whether these views are justified, and if they might be harmful in any way.

- Ask the children to imagine waking to discover they are a different gender. Ask them to list three words to describe their feelings. Using thesauruses and dictionaries, ask pupils to find another word of a similar meaning for each word they have chosen. Pupils could then write a diary extract describing their feelings.

- Get pupils to write a paragraph describing what they think will happen when Bill walks past Mean Malcolm. Encourage pupils to try to write in the same style as the extract.

- Split the class into small groups and ask each group to write a playscript based around the issues in *Bill's New Frock*. They should write about waking up and discovering that they are a different gender, and what happens as they go about their daily life. Make sure the groups are evenly split so that they are writing about girls turning into boys as well as boys turning into girls.

Let's Get Growing!

Question Book:
Year 3, pages 10-11

Author / Source:
Chris Collins and Lia Leendertz

Genre:
Non-fiction — persuasive text

Cross-curricular links:

• Science (bees and pollination)

• PSHE (growing your own food)

• D&T (designing a garden)

Introduction

This book is published by the Royal Horticultural Society (RHS). The RHS encourages people to "grow your own" because it believes in knowing where your food comes from, being self-sufficient and eating healthily. This book aims to introduce children to these principles and to encourage them to get out into the garden by showing them how much fun gardening can be.

Answers

1. The font is larger and in bold. E.g. It's the introduction to the rest of the text, so this makes it stand out, and helps the reader learn what the text is going to be about.

2. E.g. Because it's fun to grow, and it's fresher and tastier than what you buy in the shops.

3. E.g. Take good care of your plants.

4. E.g. They really like gardening. They say that it's "so exciting" to grow plants, and they say that growing things is "fun".

5. E.g. To persuade more people to take up gardening.

6. Any appropriate answer. E.g. Yes, because it can be very rewarding. For example, you can grow your own herbs and vegetables to eat, and you can enjoy being outdoors at the same time.

Extra Activities

• Discuss as a class what features suggest this extract is a persuasive text. You might want to discuss the use of rhetorical questions to encourage children to do what the author is suggesting, or exclamation marks to make what the author is saying more exciting.

• Invite pupils to turn this extract into a poster which aims to interest people in gardening. Ask them to condense the text so the poster gets across the main messages contained in the extract. They should think about layout, colour and use of images in order to make the poster look as appealing as possible.

• As a class, or in groups, research the role of bees and other insects in helping plants reproduce through pollination. Explain how pollinators are in decline, but how gardeners can help by planting flowers rich in pollen and nectar. Research the types of plants that are best for this.

• Split the class into groups of three and give each child a topic — knowing where your food comes from, being self-sufficient, and eating healthily. Introduce the topics beforehand, and then ask the pupils to discuss them in their groups.

• Ask pupils to research different varieties of fruit, vegetables and pollen-rich flowers that can be grown in British gardens. Give each pupil a piece of A4 paper and ask them to design their own garden, including some of the plants that they have found out about. Ask them to annotate their gardens to explain the reasons for their choices.

Daddy Fell into the Pond

Question Book:
Year 3, pages 12-13

Author / Source:
Alfred Noyes

Genre:
Classic poetry

Cross-curricular links:
*   Drama (performance)

Introduction

Alfred Noyes (1880-1958) was an English writer and poet. He is best known for his ballad, *The Highwayman*. *Daddy Fell into the Pond* is a comic poem which was first published in 1952. The characters' dull mood at the start of the poem is lifted when "Daddy" falls into the pond. As you read the poem with the class, ask them to pay particular attention to Noyes' use of rhythm and rhyme.

Answers

1. E.g. No. They are grumbling and they don't have anything to do.

2. E.g. To show how bored everyone is.

3. E.g. To show that something important and completely different is about to happen.

4. E.g. The noise the camera makes when the photograph is taken.

5. E.g. He felt amused. You can tell because he "slapped his knee" and he shook with laughter.

6. beyond and respond (1 mark for both correct)

7. Any appropriate answer. E.g. I think I would laugh and try to take a photo. Then I might try to help the person to get out of the pond and check that they are okay.

Extra Activities

*   With the whole class, explore the rhythm of the poem. What is the rhythm like at the start of the poem? How does it change after "Daddy" falls into the pond? How do the changes in rhythm mirror changes in the characters' moods?

*   As a class, identify all the rhyming words in the poem. Split the class into groups and assign each group a rhyme from the poem. Ask them to come up with as many words as possible that have the same rhyme.

*   Ask pupils to come up with their own poem which starts with a dull atmosphere and features an amusing event and a mood shift. They should try and use rhyming couplets and triplets, like in *Daddy Fell into the Pond*.

*   Ask the class to write a story based on the poem's events, from the father's perspective. Ask them to include details about the setting, the characters, why everyone is so bored, how he fell into the pond and his reaction to falling in and everyone laughing at him.

*   Split the class into groups and ask them to stage a performance of the poem. One person in each group should be the narrator, while the others act out the poem. Encourage pupils to think about how they can convey the suddenness of the father falling into the pond.

The Demon Headmaster

Question Book:
Year 3, pages 14-15

Author / Source:
Gillian Cross

Genre:
Fiction — novel extract

Cross-curricular links:
*   Maths (multiplication)
*   Geography (Europe)

Introduction

The Demon Headmaster is the first in a series of seven books by the award-winning children's author Gillian Cross. This book focuses on Dinah Glass and her foster brothers, Lloyd and Harvey, as they try to put a stop to the Headmaster's evil plot to take over the country and subject it to a merciless system of order and discipline. In this extract, Dinah attends her new school for the first time. She is surprised by the other pupils' strange behaviour, which she later learns is a symptom of the Headmaster's sinister influence over the school. Before reading the text with the class, ask pupils to list their favourite playground activities.

Answers

1. E.g. Because she is new to the school and she doesn't know anyone.

2. E.g. She expects them to play games, shout and tell jokes.

3. E.g. Because they aren't doing any of the things she expects. Instead, they are standing in small groups and talking quietly.

4. d. serious

5. E.g. Because they don't stop reciting or turn around, even though Dinah is standing beside them.

6. E.g. She feels scared. It might be because she thinks someone will tell her off.

Extra Activities

*   With the whole class, ask pupils to compare the behaviour of the children in *The Demon Headmaster* with the playground activities they listed before reading the extract. Are the activities they enjoy similar or different? Do they find the children's behaviour surprising? Ask pupils to suggest a variety of possible explanations for the children's behaviour.

*   Ask pupils to identify the feelings that Dinah, Lucy and Julie experience over the course of the extract. Get pupils to identify the words and phrases that convey these feelings, and encourage them to explain why the characters feel the way they do.

*   Ask pupils to write a paragraph describing what they think happens next in the story.

*   Get pupils to write a letter from Dinah to a friend, describing Dinah's first day at school. Writing from Dinah's perspective, they should use their own words to describe the experiences and feelings mentioned in the extract.

*   Challenge pupils to work out the 21 times table up to 10 x 21. ⟶ 21, 42, 63, 84, 105, 126, 147, 168, 189, 210

*   Give pupils a map of Europe and a list of ten European countries. Ask them to label the ten countries on their maps, using an atlas or online map to help them if necessary. They should then find out the capital cities of each of the countries they have labelled and mark these on their maps too. Finally, pupils should find out the capital of the United States.

Robotic Baby Penguin

Question Book:
Year 3, pages 16-17

Author / Source:
www.independent.co.uk

Genre:
Non-fiction — news article

Cross-curricular links:
- Science (penguins; robots)
- D&T (designing a robot)

Introduction

Robotics is a relatively new discipline, but one that has been developing rapidly in recent decades. Robots are now being used to perform an increasingly wide range of tasks, from industrial processes to domestic chores. This article focuses on the use of robots in scientific research, describing a robotic rover, containing a camera, which is designed to look like a penguin chick. This fluffy robot is able to approach emperor penguins without scaring them, allowing researchers to observe their behaviour from much closer than was previously possible. Before pupils read the text, ask them what they think of when they hear the word 'robot'.

Answers

1. E.g. Because the penguins are shy and run away from the researchers. The robot can get closer to the penguins without scaring them away.

2. d. an adverb

3. Adelie Land in Antarctica

4. bot

5. E.g. Difficult. The text says that the first version of the robot scared the real penguins away, and the scientists had to try several different designs before they made a robot they could use.

6. E.g. Because it didn't answer them when they sang to it.

7. Any appropriate answer. E.g. I think he felt happy and relieved that his team had finally designed a robot that could get close to the penguins. He might also have felt excited about what he would be able to find out about the penguins using the robot.

Extra Activities

- Ask pupils to briefly summarise the information in the article by writing a few words under each of the following headings: 'who', 'what', 'where' and 'why'.

- As a class, discuss how the robot in the article compares with pupils' existing ideas about robots.

- Ask pupils to research emperor penguins and produce a poster about them. Their poster should include pictures of both an adult emperor penguin and a chick, as well as information about the penguins' habitat, diet and behaviour.

- Explain that robots are now used to perform a wide range of tasks, many of which were once done by humans. Show pupils pictures or videos of robots from a variety of fields (e.g. car production, bomb disposal, deep-sea exploration), and discuss why robots are better suited than humans to these roles.

- Ask pupils to design a robot that would be able to carry out their favourite hobby with them. They should draw an annotated diagram of their robot, showing the tasks it is able to perform, and the special features it has which enable it to perform those tasks.

High Adventure

Question Book:
Year 3, pages 18-19

Author / Source:
Sir Edmund Hillary

Genre:
Non-fiction — memoir

Cross-curricular links:
*   Art (illustrating a text)
*   Geography (tourism)
*   Maths (ordering numbers)

Introduction

On 29 May 1953, Edmund Hillary and Tenzing Norgay made history when they became the first people to reach the summit of Mount Everest. In this extract, Hillary describes how he fell in love with mountains when he went on his first skiing holiday at the age of sixteen. Before pupils read the extract, make sure they read the introduction so that they are aware of Hillary's subsequent career as one of the twentieth century's most famous mountaineers.

Answers

1. E.g. Because he had never been very far from Auckland before, and he wanted to see the world.

2. E.g. He felt excited and happy because he was seeing snow for the first time — he says it was "a tremendous thrill".

3. "as hard as iron"

4. E.g. Because it makes the mountain sound magical, like in a fairy tale, and helps you imagine how beautiful it was.

5. E.g. Because he had been told that they were dangerous. OR Because he was scared of them.

6. Any appropriate answer. E.g. Yes, because this ski trip was the first time that he saw snow and mountains. It gave him a "fiery enthusiasm" for them, which probably made him want to be a mountaineer.

Extra Activities

*   With the whole class, discuss the conventions of autobiographies and memoirs, encouraging pupils to identify features of this text which show that it is an example of autobiographical writing.

*   Get pupils to write a short autobiographical passage or memoir describing the first time they did a favourite activity.

*   Focusing on lines 11-18, ask pupils to identify the techniques that Hillary uses to describe the mountains. With the whole class, discuss the way these techniques help to build up a vivid image of the scene.

*   Ask pupils to suggest other ways to describe a snowy scene. Get them to write and illustrate their own short passage, using descriptive language to create a vivid image of a snowy scene.

*   Using the information in the extract, their own imaginations and online research if possible, get pupils to create a tourist brochure that will persuade people to visit Ruapehu. They may want to include a description of the natural beauty of the volcano, and suggestions for activities that people could do during their visit.

*   Give pupils an alphabetical list of the ten highest mountains in the world and their heights in metres. Challenge pupils to arrange the list into height order.

Annapurna I — 8091 m
Cho Oyu — 8188 m
Dhaulagiri I — 8167 m
Everest — 8848 m
K2 — 8611 m
Kangchenjunga — 8586 m
Lhotse — 8516 m
Makalu — 8485 m
Manaslu — 8163 m
Nanga Parbat — 8126 m

An Interview with Rebecca Adlington

Question Book:
Year 3, pages 20-21

Author / Source:
http://www.nhs.uk

Genre:
Non-fiction — interview

Cross-curricular links:
*   Science (nutrition)
*   PSHE (setting goals)

Introduction

Rebecca Adlington is a former competitive swimmer and one of Great Britain's most successful female Olympic athletes. She won two gold medals at the 2008 Olympics in Beijing, where she also broke the world record for the women's 800 m freestyle. In 2012, she won two bronze medals at the London Olympics. In this interview, conducted in 2010, Rebecca talks about how she first started swimming, why she loves the sport, and her advice for staying motivated.

Answers

1. E.g. So that they wouldn't be worried about her when she went in the pool on holiday.

2. E.g. Because both old people and young people can go swimming.

3. about 25 hours

4. E.g. She really enjoys swimming, and she likes competing with other people.

5. c. swim with people of different ages

6. E.g. Yes. When she was younger, she would try to swim as fast as her sisters, and she says that competing with the other people in her squad helps to motivate her.

7. Any appropriate answer. E.g. Yes, because it says lots of good things about swimming. For example, it says that swimming is "fun" and that it's good for you.

Extra Activities

*   Ask pupils to identify phrases from lines 11-20 of the text that might persuade people to start swimming. Get them to suggest other persuasive phrases to encourage participation in their own favourite sports.

*   Adlington won two silver medals at the European Youth Olympic Festival in 2003. Ask pupils to write a diary entry from Adlington's perspective, just after the competition. They should describe her feelings about the competition, and explain why it motivated her to dedicate herself to competitive swimming.

*   As a class, discuss the sacrifices that young athletes, particularly those of school age, have to make in order to train to a competitive standard. Why do they think people make these sacrifices? Have pupils ever had to make similar sacrifices in order to work towards something they wanted to achieve?

*   Explain that eating a healthy, balanced diet is important to enable us to participate in sports like swimming, as well as all the other activities we do every day. Give pupils pictures of a variety of different foods, and ask them to sort them into the correct food groups (carbohydrates, proteins, etc.). Get pupils to invent some meals which include at least one ingredient from each of the food groups.

*   Get pupils to write down a realistic goal (either academic or physical) that they would like to achieve in the next two to four weeks, and a plan for how they can work towards it. Ask pupils for regular updates on their progress, and celebrate the success of those who achieve their goals.

My Name is Mina

Question Book:
Year 3, pages 22-23

Author / Source:
David Almond

Genre:
Fiction — novel extract

Cross-curricular links:
•   Art (illustrating imagery)
•   Science (the mind)

Introduction

My Name is Mina, first published in 2010, is the prequel to David Almond's *Skellig* — a very popular children's novel. Written in the form of a diary, *My Name is Mina* gives the reader a first-hand insight into nine-year-old Mina's unique view of the world. In this extract, Mina starts writing her diary, and explores what words and storytelling mean to her. Rich in similes, metaphors and other literary devices, this extract provides an ideal opportunity for pupils to start exploring creative writing and its effect on the reader.

Answers

1.   Night-time. E.g. You can tell because there's moonlight.

2.   E.g. To show how Mina wrote the words in her diary.

3.   E.g. She means a blank page with no words written on it.

4.   E.g. It would only have one word written on it.

5.   c. a collective noun

6.   E.g. Because the way she thinks isn't organised and tidy like straight lines — it's messy and disorganised.

7.   Any appropriate answer. E.g. Imaginative. The way she writes shows that she sees lots of interesting images in her mind, and she uses language in creative ways to help the reader see those images too.

Extra Activities

•   As a class, discuss the characteristic features of diary entries. What features does Mina's diary have in common with more conventional diaries? In what ways is it different?

•   In this extract, Mina uses imaginative imagery to describe the way animals move (e.g. "flicker like bats"). Get pupils to think of other animals that they are familiar with, and challenge them to think of verbs to describe the way they move. Encourage them to be creative in their suggestions.

•   Explain that in the phrase "a swirling swarm of starlings", the author has deliberately chosen words that start with the same 's' sound. Give pupils a list of collective nouns for other groups of animals, and ask them to suggest alliterative phrases to describe them (e.g. a fluttering flamboyance of flamingos).

•   The language in this extract creates vivid images in the reader's mind. Focusing on lines 5-21, ask pupils to identify examples of imagery, such as similes, and to describe the pictures that they create. Get pupils to choose an example of imagery, and ask them to draw a picture to represent it.

•   Ask pupils to write an opening paragraph for their own diary that uses language creatively.

•   Mina describes the mind as "a place of wonder". As a class, explore why the mind might be viewed in this way. Make sure pupils are aware that their minds control both their mental and their physical functions, and encourage them to explore all the things that their minds enable them to do.

Poems about Crocodiles

Question Book:
Year 3, pages 24-25

Author / Source:
Lewis Carroll
Christine F. Fletcher

Genre:
Poetry

Cross-curricular links:
• Science (Nile crocodiles)

Introduction

These two poems on the subject of crocodiles were written approximately a century apart. Lewis Carroll's *How Doth the Little Crocodile* appears in his novel, *Alice's Adventures in Wonderland*, which was first published in 1865. *If You Should Meet a Crocodile* was written by Christine F. Fletcher during an English lesson when she was at secondary school in 1957. It was originally published without her knowledge, and she has only recently been acknowledged as its author. The two poems offer many points of comparison, both in their subject matter, and in the language and poetic techniques they use, giving pupils plenty of scope to explore similarities and differences between them.

Answers

1. the third person

2. Nile

3. a. to grin b. smile

4. thinner

5. E.g. He is eating the "little fishes".

6. E.g. Because the crocodile is always hungry, and if you disturb him, he might eat you.

7. Any appropriate answer. E.g. No, because he's only little, and words like "gently smiling" make him sound friendly rather than frightening.

Extra Activities

• With the whole class, compare the rhyme schemes of the two poems, encouraging pupils to identify similarities and differences between them. Get pupils to pick out the pairs or groups of words that rhyme in each poem, and ask them to think of as many other words as they can that would also rhyme.

• Make sure pupils understand what a syllable is, then get them to count the number of syllables in each line of *How Doth the Little Crocodile*. Can they spot a pattern? How many syllables are there in each line of *If You Should Meet a Crocodile*? How does this pattern compare with *How Doth the Little Crocodile*?

• Ask pupils to choose a wild animal and write their own eight-line poem describing what you should do if you meet that animal. They should follow the rhyme scheme and pattern of syllables used in *If You Should Meet a Crocodile*.

• Get pupils to find another poem about an animal that they enjoy. Pupils should read the poem they have chosen to the class and explain why they like it.

• Ask pupils to research the Nile crocodile and produce an informative poster covering information such as how large this species of crocodile can grow, where it lives and what it eats.

The Secret History of Tom Trueheart

Question Book:
Year 3, pages 26-27

Author / Source:
Ian Beck

Genre:
Fiction — novel extract

Cross-curricular links:
- Art (cartoon strip)
- PSHE (being different)

Introduction

The Secret History of Tom Trueheart is the first in a series of three fantasy novels by Ian Beck. The hero of these novels, Tom Trueheart, comes from a family of fairy-tale heroes, but unlike his adventurous brothers, Tom considers himself to be a coward. In this engaging extract, Beck uses descriptive language to bring his characters to life. Before reading the text with the class, discuss what a fairy tale is and the typical features you would expect to find in one. Ask pupils to make a list of all the fairy tales they are familiar with.

Answers

1. fables

2. E.g. It tells you that the story is set a long time ago.

3. eight

4. E.g. Because they are involved in lots of daring and exciting adventures.

5. Any two from: Tom is not tall, but his brothers are; Tom is "wiry", but his brothers are "broad"; Tom has curly hair, but his brothers have straight hair.

6. E.g. No, because he finds them scary, and they give him nightmares.

7. E.g. Everyone in Tom's family is brave, so maybe he is embarrassed that he isn't brave too. He might be worried that they wouldn't like him if they knew he wasn't brave.

Extra Activities

- As a class, compare the extract with the pupils' list of typical features of fairy tales. In what ways is the extract similar to other fairy tales pupils have read? How is it different?

- Focusing on lines 1-15, ask pupils to identify all the adjectives that Ian Beck uses to describe members of the Trueheart family. Challenge them to think of an antonym for each adjective.

- With the whole class, discuss what the *Land of Stories* might be like. Ask pupils to suggest characters and places from stories they've read that you might find in the *Land of Stories*. Get pupils to write a short story set in the *Land of Stories*, drawing on the ideas raised in the discussion and their own imaginations.

- Ask pupils to imagine an exciting adventure experienced by one of Tom's brothers. Get them to create a cartoon strip showing the adventure.

- Tom Trueheart is very different from other members of his family. With the whole class, discuss how this might make him feel. Have pupils ever experienced feeling different or like they don't fit in? How did they cope with this? What could Tom's brothers do to make sure that being different isn't a problem for Tom?

Jellyfish in the UK

Question Book:
Year 3, pages 28-29

Author / Source:
www.independent.co.uk

Genre:
Non-fiction — news article

Cross-curricular links:
- Science (grouping animals)
- Art (making a collage)

Introduction

Jellyfish are found throughout the world's oceans. They are among some of the oldest animals in the world, and their anatomy is very simple. They don't have specialised digestive, respiratory or circulatory systems, and instead of a brain, they have a simple nervous system called a 'nerve net'. Jellyfish swim by pulsating their bell-shaped bodies, and they use their stinging tentacles to catch prey. This news article introduces pupils to the barrel jellyfish, a harmless species sometimes found off the British coast. Before pupils read the article, show them some pictures of barrel jellyfish.

Answers

1. E.g. lots; tons; loads

2. E.g. Because they eat plankton, and plankton grow really well when the weather is warm.

3. a brain and bones

4. E.g. Because they swim deeper in the winter and go further away from the UK.

5. a. factual

6. E.g. It has a large headline, and it's written in columns.

7. Any appropriate answer. E.g. He might have been excited because he says that it's the biggest barrel jellyfish he's seen. However, he might also have been scared because it seems like it appeared out of nowhere and the size of it might have frightened him.

Extra Activities

- Ask pupils to write a postcard from Todd Palmer, the diver mentioned in the article, to a friend, describing his encounter with the barrel jellyfish and explaining how it made him feel.

- This text is an example of a news article. Show pupils some more news articles and discuss the conventions that they follow. Are there any features that all the articles have in common? Which features only appear in some of the articles? Encourage pupils to think about the purpose of the various features they have identified.

- Ask pupils to write their own news article, reporting a recent school event (e.g. sports day, a class trip or a school fair). They should use some of the news article conventions identified in the class discussion.

- Explain the difference between vertebrates and invertebrates, and tell pupils that jellyfish are a type of invertebrate. Divide the class into groups and give each group pictures of some other animals. Challenge pupils to identify the animals and find out which are vertebrates and which are invertebrates. As a class, discuss other ways that the animals could be grouped.

- Get pupils to create a collage showing an underwater scene. Encourage them to use a variety of different materials to give their collage texture and colour.

Carrie's War

Question Book:
Year 3, pages 30-31

Author / Source:
Nina Bawden

Genre:
Fiction — novel extract

Cross-curricular links:
- History (evacuation)
- PSHE (family relationships)

Introduction

Carrie's War by Nina Bawden is considered a modern classic. Set during World War Two, it tells the story of two siblings, Carrie and Nick, who are evacuated to Wales from their home in London. The novel begins with Carrie revisiting Wales with her own children thirty years later, where she tells them the story of what happened while she was an evacuee there. Nina Bawden lived in Wales as an evacuee herself, and was influenced by this experience when she wrote the novel. Make sure pupils know that the novel is set during World War Two, and explain the term 'evacuation' and why it was common during the war.

Answers

1. "Such a noise" OR "it seemed to split the sky open" OR "Enough to frighten the dead"

2. E.g. No, because she mops his face with her handkerchief and calls him "Poor lamb".

3. E.g. To make him feel better because he seemed upset about leaving home.

4. a. E.g. To feel pleased with yourself. b. E.g. Because she was correct about Nick being sick.

5. E.g. She's a teacher at Carrie's school.

6. Any appropriate answer. E.g. Because she wants to make the countryside sound nice so that Nick and Carrie won't be upset about leaving home.

7. Any appropriate answer. E.g. I think they would have felt scared to leave home and go somewhere they didn't know. I think they also would have felt sad to leave without their family.

Extra Activities

- The last question in the Question Book asks pupils how Carrie and Nick would have felt being evacuated. As a class, discuss pupils' answers. Ask them to imagine that they are about to be evacuated themselves and to write a diary entry about their feelings as if it is the night before they are about to leave home.

- Ask the children to imagine that they have arrived at their new home in the countryside. Get them to write a letter home to their parents, telling them how they are finding life so far. This should be a continuation of the character they created for their diary entry. Their feelings about evacuation may have changed now that they've arrived in the countryside, or they may have stayed the same.

- Find some letters on the Internet from real evacuees during the war and read them as a class. Compare the real letters with the pupils' imagined ones and discuss the similarities and differences between them.

- Split the class into groups and get each group to research a different aspect of evacuation, e.g. why it was introduced, who was evacuated, how they were evacuated. Each group should present their findings to the rest of the class.

- As a class, discuss what they have learnt about Carrie and Nick's relationship from the extract. Invite pupils to compare Carrie and Nick's relationship with the relationships within their own families.

Choosing a Bike

Question Book:
Year 4, pages 2-3

Author / Source:
www.nhs.uk/change4life

Genre:
Non-fiction — reference text

Cross-curricular links:
- PSHE (healthy lifestyle; bike safety)
- D&T (bike design)

Introduction

This extract about choosing the right bike is from the *Change4Life* programme — a campaign by the NHS to promote healthy living. Pupils may have seen adverts as part of this campaign on national television. The campaign aims to help and encourage people to eat well, drink less alcohol and exercise more. The extract is an informative text, but it also contains elements of persuasive writing.

Answers

1. Any one from: it makes cycling easier; it makes cycling safer; or it makes cycling more fun.

2. Because you can use them on roads and on rough tracks.

3. E.g. Something created from two different things. Hybrid is a suitable name because hybrid bikes are a cross between a road bike and a cross-country mountain bike.

4. E.g. They have suspension.

5. E.g. Mountain bikes can be ridden on rough tracks and the suspension cushions these bumps. However, racing bikes are only used for riding on the road where the surface isn't as rough.

6. E.g. A racing bike owner, because racing bikes don't have very comfortable seats.

7. Any appropriate answer. E.g. I would choose a hybrid bike because they are "very comfortable". Also, I haven't done very much cycling, so I would choose a hybrid bike because they're good for beginners.

Extra Activities

- Ask pupils in groups to make a list of the advantages of cycling over other modes of transport, and then, as a class, discuss their ideas. Ask pupils to imagine they have been asked to create a poster for the *Change4Life* campaign to encourage people to take up cycling. They should use the ideas they have discussed and focus on making their poster as persuasive as possible.

- Have a look at the *Change4Life* website, and, as a class, discuss the importance of leading a healthy lifestyle. Ask pupils why they think the NHS wants people to live healthier lives.

- Ask pupils to explain their answers to question 7 in the Question Book. Are any of them keen cyclists or interested in cycling? Discuss the importance of bike safety (e.g. wearing a helmet and high-visibility clothing) and maintenance (checking that the tyres and chain are in good condition).

- Divide the class into groups, and give each group a top British cyclist to research. Pupils should use their findings to write an informative fact sheet about their given cyclist. → *Victoria Pendleton, Bradley Wiggins, Chris Hoy, Nicole Cooke, Chris Froome*

- Split the class into small groups. Each group should be given a picture of either a mountain bike, a hybrid bike or a racing bike. They should label the distinctive features on each bike and research why these features are useful, e.g. thin tyres help bikes go faster, suspension cushions bumps.

The Tale of Custard the Dragon

Question Book:
Year 4, pages 4-5

Author / Source:
Ogden Nash

Genre:
Classic poetry

Cross-curricular links:
- PSHE (courage; friendship)
- Drama (performance)

Introduction

The American poet Ogden Nash (1902-1971) was a popular writer of light verse — poetry which entertains its readers through the use of nonsense and word play. *The Tale of Custard the Dragon* tells the story of a dragon who is teased for being cowardly, but one day proves that he can be brave. Ogden wrote a sequel to this poem called *Custard the Dragon and the Wicked Knight*, in which Custard again demonstrates his bravery. Before reading the poem with the class, it may be useful to explain to pupils that the word 'custard' is associated with cowardliness.

Answers

1. E.g. The kitten's fur is black, which is the usual colour of pen ink.

2. E.g. He has big sharp teeth, spikes on his back and scales on his stomach, he breathes fire, snorts smoke and has very sharp claws.

3. E.g. Because his mouth is full of flames like a fireplace.

4. E.g. So that it rhymes with "Belinda" on the previous line.

5. E.g. The blood has gone from her face because she is scared.

6. E.g. To hold something close. It shows she is thankful to Custard for saving them.

7. Any appropriate answer. E.g. He might feel happy that he has saved his friends and that they are so grateful. However, he's still scared of the outside world, so he still doesn't have much confidence.

Extra Activities

- Discuss the poem's form. Can pupils see that the poem is written in 4-line stanzas and rhyming couplets?

- Introduce the term 'light verse' to the class, and together, identify and discuss features of light verse in the poem. E.g. Discuss why the poet uses the made-up words and phrases "realio, trulio" and "pyrate", and what effect they have. Explore the way the poet uses similes and metaphors in the poem too.

- Ask pupils to write and illustrate two of their own stanzas, modelling them on the first two stanzas of *The Tale of Custard the Dragon*. They should introduce a new setting with different pets which have different names and follow the same rhyme scheme.

- In pairs, ask pupils to discuss the message of the poem. Has there been a time when they have done something they thought they wouldn't be able to do? Is there something that they would like to do but are scared to try?

- As a class, discuss how Custard is treated by his friends. What do pupils think about this treatment?

- Split the class into groups and ask them to prepare and perform a version of the poem. Get them to focus on using their voices and actions to express the emotions and events in the poem.

Aesop's Fables

Question Book:
Year 4, pages 6-7

Author / Source:
Aesop

Genre:
Fiction — fables

Cross-curricular links:
• History (life of Aesop)
• PSHE (relating to others)

Introduction

Aesop's Fables are a collection of short stories which contain a moral message. They are credited to Aesop, who is said to have been a slave who lived in Ancient Greece around 600 BC. However, it is possible that these stories have come from various sources and that they have just been attributed to Aesop — some scholars even dispute his existence.

Answers

1. E.g. The Fox wants to have some fun and play a trick on the Stork.

2. E.g. Because he has a calm personality and doesn't see the point in getting angry.

3. E.g. He treats the Fox in the same way that the Fox treated him. By serving him dinner in a jar that only the Stork can eat from, the Stork shows the Fox that his behaviour was unacceptable.

4. E.g. Crafty; sneaky; cunning. The Fox is being sly because he's thinking of a plan to take the cheese from the Crow so that he can eat it himself.

5. E.g. Because the Fox is saying nice things to her, so she starts to trust and believe him.

6. E.g. Don't always trust people who say nice things to you.

7. E.g. Foxes are known for being sly and cunning creatures, and in both fables, the Fox's character does sly and cunning things.

Extra Activities

• Identify and discuss with the class the fable form and how it differs from other fiction texts they may have read. You may want to discuss animal characters who behave like humans; simple settings and characters; and a lack of descriptive language etc.

• Give the class these three morals: 'Those who try to please everyone please no-one', 'A liar will not be believed, even when he tells the truth' and 'One good turn deserves another'. Ask them to choose one and write their own fable to match the moral.

• Find some fables on the Internet, and read them with the class without giving them the moral. Ask pupils what they think the morals of the fables are. ⟶

The Tortoise and the Hare
The Crow and the Pitcher
The Fox and the Goat

• Split the class into groups and ask them to research Aesop. Make sure they are aware that Aesop may not have come up with all the fables himself and that he might not have even existed. Pupils should use their findings to write an informative fact sheet about Aesop.

• Discuss the morals of the two fables with the class. Why do they think they should be aware of flattery? Why is it important to treat others as they would want to be treated? Can they think of a modern-day scenario where these morals may apply? Can they apply the morals to their own experiences?

An Interview with Jacqueline Wilson

Question Book:
Year 4, pages 8-9

Author / Source:
https://clubs-kids.scholastic.co.uk

Genre:
Non-fiction — interview

Cross-curricular links:
*   PSHE (personal achievements)
*   Science (dreams)
*   Art (book cover)

Introduction

Jacqueline Wilson, born in 1945, is a very popular children's author. A former British Children's Laureate, it is likely that many pupils will have heard of her and will be familiar with her books. She addresses challenging issues in her books, such as children in care in *Tracy Beaker,* and mental illness in *The Illustrated Mum* — two of her books which are mentioned in the interview. Tracy Beaker is probably her best-known character, and some pupils may also be familiar with the *Tracy Beaker* television series.

Answers

1. 22

2. E.g. She wasn't writing in the way that teachers wanted her to write.

3. E.g. It turned out how she had hoped it would, which doesn't happen often when she writes books.

4. E.g. In the same way that you don't know where your dreams come from or what they're going to be, she doesn't know where her ideas are going to come from or what they're going to be.

5. E.g. She was looking at all the things in her bathroom, and when she looked at a beaker, it gave her the idea for the surname.

6. E.g. It's been a success, and it's been written just the way she would have written it.

7. Any appropriate answer. E.g. Exciting, because you're popular and successful. It might also be a challenge because it must be difficult having to come up with lots of good ideas for books and write them.

Extra Activities

*   Ask pupils to write a newspaper article on Jacqueline Wilson's writing career and her success with *Tracy Beaker*. They can use the information from the interview, as well as doing their own research.

*   Discuss with the class how ideas and inspiration can come from anywhere. Ask the pupils to plan their own short story, coming up with a main character, setting and other characters. They should plan a beginning, a middle and an end for their story, and then write it.

*   Split the class into pairs and ask each pupil to think of something they have achieved in their lives. Pupils should take it in turns to interview their partner about their achievement and how it made them feel.

*   As a class, discuss dreams and where they come from, e.g. some scientists believe that dreaming is the brain's way of sorting through information it collects during the day. Split the class into small groups and ask them to discuss their own dreams. Can they remember their dreams? What's the strangest thing they've ever dreamt about? Can they make any links between their dreams and real life?

*   Jacqueline Wilson's books have very distinctive cover art, created by the artist Nick Sharratt. Show the class some examples of these covers and ask the pupils to come up with their own cover designs for the story they planned and wrote in the second activity.

Harry Drinkwater's Diary

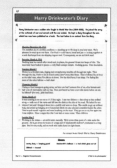

Question Book:
Year 4, pages 10-11

Author / Source:
Harry Drinkwater

Genre:
Non-fiction — diary

Cross-curricular links:
*   History (World War One; sources)
*   Art (war paintings)

Introduction

Harry Drinkwater served as a front-line soldier throughout World War One. He was initially rejected by the army for being too short, but managed to join the Birmingham Pals Battalion. He later became an officer and was awarded the Military Cross. Even though soldiers weren't allowed to keep diaries, he kept one for the duration of the war, storing it in his tunic pocket. He fought in the Somme and Passchendaele, witnessing many of his friends being killed, but miraculously managing to survive the war himself. He died in 1978.

Answers

1. E.g. Because of the rain.

2. E.g. Because muddy water drips from the roof onto the sack containing their food.

3. E.g. Frantic; frenzied; very fast. They worked as fast as they could to try to get the job done.

4. E.g. He's so tired because they're working hard with very little sleep.

5. E.g. Because the food transports got lost and didn't arrive.

6. E.g. He was very tired and needed help from others to stand up. He tried to keep moving, but he collapsed with exhaustion.

7. E.g. Because it must have been unpleasant being underground and having to work in stuffy conditions. It would have been dark and cramped, and the work would have been dangerous, tiring and difficult.

Extra Activities

*   Split the class into groups and ask them to research a different aspect of the trenches that are touched on in Harry's diary, e.g. food that soldiers ate, their daily routine, illnesses, mines and tunnel warfare. Get them to create an informative poster which they can present to the rest of the class.

*   Ask pupils to imagine that they are soldiers fighting in the trenches. Get them to write letters home talking about their experiences.

*   Explain that Harry's diaries were bought by a man at an auction and have now been published as a book. Ask pupils why they think this source is valuable and why it is important for people to read it.

*   Split the class into groups and ask them to research what the trenches looked like. Get them to produce large annotated diagrams on a poster which show the allied and enemy trenches, No Man's Land, barbed-wire defences, and smaller details such as sandbags and planks which reinforced the trenches.

*   Show the pupils paintings which reflect Harry's diary e.g. *The Menin Road* and *We are Making a New World* by Paul Nash and *Reliefs at Dawn*, *March of Civilisation* and *After a Push* by Christopher Nevinson. Discuss as a class how these paintings reflect Harry's experience, what the pupils think the paintings are trying to show and how the paintings make them feel.

Hamish and the Worldstoppers

Question Book:
Year 4, pages 12-13

Author / Source:
Danny Wallace

Genre:
Fiction — novel extract

Cross-curricular links:
- Drama (performance)
- Science (time zones)

Introduction

Hamish and the Worldstoppers is by Danny Wallace, an author, presenter, actor, comedian and filmmaker. The book is about a boy called Hamish who decides to have some fun when one day, the world and everything in it suddenly stops, except for him. However, he soon discovers that the world has stopped because of some monsters who want to take over the world, and it's up to Hamish to stop them. Ensure pupils have read the introduction before they answer question 6 in the Question Book.

Answers

1. E.g. They are opened wide because he's surprised and shocked by what's happening.

2. E.g. It emphasises the narrator's confusion and the fact that he wants to know what is going on.

3. E.g. "scariest" and "coolest"

4. 'Incredibly' and 'weird'. E.g. It means that something is extraordinarily strange.

5. E.g. 'Blather' means to talk for a long time without saying anything meaningful, and 'Long' emphasises this. The author wants to show that the teacher is boring and talks endlessly.

6. E.g. Everything in the world, except for Hamish, has stopped.

7. Any appropriate answer. E.g. Yes, because you know that something strange has happened, but the last paragraph doesn't explain it, so it makes me want to keep reading to find out what has happened.

Extra Activities

- Discuss the inventive and humorous language used by Wallace in the extract, e.g. combining two words to make the word '*incredi*-weird' and making up names which reflect characters such as Mr Longblather. Ask pupils to make up their own words to describe how they'd feel if time froze, and to come up with names to describe people such as a nosy neighbour, a snobby uncle and a clumsy friend.

- Ask the class to imagine that they are sat in a classroom when the world suddenly stops. Ask volunteers to tell the rest of the class what they would do, and encourage other pupils to ask them questions about their choice. Drawing on the class discussion, pupils could then write a diary entry describing what was happening when time froze and how they reacted.

- Split the class into groups and get them to act out different scenarios of time freezing, e.g. at a supermarket checkout or during a swimming lesson. One pupil in each group should be the main character, another the narrator and the rest extras. Ask pupils to swap roles and scenarios so that each gets a turn at being the main character or the narrator.

- Explain to the class the different time zones around the world. Challenge pupils to find out what time it is in different cities across the globe. *New York, Paris, Moscow, Dubai, Sydney*

BBC Women's Footballer of the Year

Question Book:
Year 4, pages 14-15

Author / Source:
www.prolificnorth.co.uk

Genre:
Non-fiction — news article

Cross-curricular links:

- PSHE (gender inequality)
- Geography (international football)
- Maths (statistics)
- PE (football tournament)

Introduction

In 2015, the BBC World Service introduced the Women's Footballer of the Year award. Five players were short-listed for the award and it was voted for by football fans from all over the world. The winner was 20-year-old Asisat Oshoala who plays for Nigeria and Liverpool Ladies, and her victory was announced at the end of May, just before the start of the 2015 Women's World Cup in early June.

Answers

1. E.g. Because people have voted for her to become BBC Women's Footballer of the Year.

2. E.g. It's a confidence boost, so she'll probably want to continue to do well.

3. E.g. Because she was very successful in 2014 — she played in the under-20s Women's World Cup and won two other awards.

4. E.g. A very impressive and skilled player who should be respected.

5. "proud" and "thrilled"

6. E.g. She was the tournament's "leading scorer", and she was "voted best player". Her impressive performance helped Nigeria to get to the final.

7. Any appropriate answer. E.g. Yes, because it's good to have an award that recognises women's football skills. The award shows an effort is being made to give more support to women's football.

Extra Activities

- Get pupils to write a letter from Asisat to a friend, describing her feelings about receiving the award.

- Ask pupils to produce an advert to publicise the award. They should focus on presenting women's football in a positive light and using language to persuade people to vote for the award.

- As a class, discuss gender inequality and the differences between women's and men's football, e.g. female football players are paid less and women's football has less media coverage. Discuss whether pupils think this is fair, and ask them to write a news article, presenting their views about it.

- Asisat Oshoala is from Nigeria and the other short-listed players are from Spain, Germany, Scotland and Brazil. Ask volunteers to show the rest of the class where these countries are on a map, and then assign each pupil a country and ask them to find out five facts about it. Collate the facts in a class display.

- Browse the Internet for statistics from the 2015 Women's World Cup in Canada. Get the class to compare how Nigeria, Spain, Germany and Brazil performed, e.g. games won, games lost, goals scored.

- Hold a class football tournament. At the end, get pupils to vote for 'Player of the Tournament' — they should write a short paragraph justifying their choice.

The Real Princess

Question Book:
Year 4, pages 16-17

Author / Source:
Hans Christian Andersen

Genre:
Classic fiction — fairy tale

Cross-curricular links:
*   Art (storyboards)
*   Drama (role-play)

Introduction

Hans Christian Andersen was born in Denmark in 1805. He was a prolific writer, and his works include plays, poems, novels and travel writing. However, he is best known around the world for his fairy tales, which have been translated into more than 125 languages. *The Real Princess*, also known as *The Princess and the Pea*, was first published in 1835. Some pupils may be familiar with the story, or with other fairy tales by Andersen. As pupils read, encourage them to think about the features which show that *The Real Princess* is a fairy tale.

Answers

1. E.g. It means to feel sad. The prince feels like this because he's been trying to find a real princess to marry but hasn't been able to find one.

2. E.g. To get shelter from the bad weather.

3. E.g. She wants to find out if the princess is a real princess, and only a real princess would feel the pea under so much bedding. She didn't want the princess to find out and pretend to have slept badly.

4. E.g. She has bruises all over her.

5. Any appropriate answer. E.g. I think he feels happy and relieved that he's finally found a real princess. He had wanted to marry a real princess, but until now, his search had been very unsuccessful.

6. Any appropriate answer. E.g. The family may have kept it as a reminder of how the prince and princess came to be married, and as evidence that the princess was a real princess.

Extra Activities

*   As a class, discuss the fairy tale genre. Get pupils to identify and make a list of the fairy tale features in *The Real Princess*. Ask pupils to summarise some other fairy tales that they are familiar with and to identify the fairy tale features they contain.

*   Ask pupils to write their own short fairy tale. Encourage them to include as many of the fairy tale features identified in the class discussion as they can.

*   Ask pupils to create a storyboard for *The Real Princess*, putting the story into their own words and drawing pictures for each stage of the story.

*   Get pupils to research the life of Hans Christian Andersen. They should write down as many facts about him as they can in a bullet-point list. Then, come back together as a class and create a class display from the information that everyone has found.

*   Ask volunteers to play the main roles in the tale. They should sit at the front of the class and the other pupils have to ask them questions about their characters. Swap the volunteers around to encourage more interpretations of the characters' emotions, and so that everyone has a go.

Chinese New Year

Question Book:
Year 4, pages 18-19

Author / Source:
Alex Fairer

Genre:
Non-fiction — reference text

Cross-curricular links:
* Art (illustrating a text)
* PSHE (different cultures)
* Maths (multiples)

Introduction

Chinese New Year is celebrated by Chinese people all over the world. Traditionally, it is a time to reunite with family and to honour gods and ancestors. People perform rites such as cleaning the entire house to rid the home of bad luck and make space for good fortune in the coming year. This text is about the Chinese calendar and the animals that represent each year. It may be helpful to explain to pupils that the Chinese animal signs are similar to the twelve signs of the zodiac.

Answers

1. 22nd February

2. the tiger

3. E.g. Feeling sympathy for other people. It's seen as a positive quality because compassionate people want to help when others are having problems.

4. E.g. The year of the dragon. The dragon is an important symbol in Chinese culture, so Chinese people believe it is lucky to be born in the year of the dragon.

5. the goat

6. the year of the rat

7. Any appropriate answer. E.g. Yes, I was born in the year of the rat, and I always have lots of energy and work hard. However, I'm not a selfish person, so I don't think my animal year is completely true for me.

Extra Activities

* Assign pupils different animals from the Chinese calendar and challenge them to think of as many synonyms as they can for each of their animals' personality traits. How many antonyms can they think of for each characteristic?

* Ask pupils to select two animals from the Chinese calendar that have contrasting characteristics. Pupils should write a short story in which these two animals are the main characters. Encourage pupils to think about the personality traits mentioned in the text and how these might affect the animals' relationship.

* Ask pupils to identify an animal not mentioned in the Chinese calendar that they think best represents their personality. Pupils should write a brief description of their personality traits and illustrate it with a drawing of their chosen animal.

* With the whole class, discuss the different festivals that pupils celebrate during the year. Encourage pupils to ask each other questions about the festivals they observe. What does the festival involve? What does it mean to them? What do they enjoy about it?

* Give pupils maths problems relating to the Chinese calendar, e.g. give them a selection of years and ask them to work out the animal for each year, or ask them to find all the years of the rooster back to 1800.

The Girl Who Walked On Air

Question Book:
Year 4, pages 20-21

Author / Source:
Emma Carroll

Genre:
Fiction — novel extract

Cross-curricular links:
- History (Victorian circus)
- PSHE (animal welfare)
- Maths (multiplication and division)
- Science (gravity)

Introduction

Emma Carroll is a writer as well as a part-time English teacher. *The Girl Who Walked On Air* is her second novel and is set in the Victorian era. It's about a girl called Louie, who works in the ticket office of Chipchase's Travelling Circus after being abandoned there as a baby. She dreams of performing on the tightrope and practises in secret, until one day she gets her chance.

Answers

1. E.g. People are more likely to want to see dangerous things.

2. E.g. He's generous and kind and cares about Louie because he lets her eat the piecrust before anyone else.

3. E.g. She says her mother left her at the circus, "the way most people forget an umbrella". This shows that Louie thinks her mother didn't care about her.

4. E.g. To show that Louie's daydreaming and that they are her thoughts.

5. E.g. Lots of people have come to see the show, so he's happy because he'll make more money.

6. E.g. Because it's an exciting routine that can't be seen at any other circus.

7. Any appropriate answer. E.g. The title of the novel suggests someone is walking on a tight-rope. This is a hint that Louie may get to perform in the circus, and that she may become a star attraction herself.

Extra Activities

- As a class, read the sentences in italics again. Ask pupils to continue writing Louie's daydream as if she hadn't been interrupted, focusing on how she would feel when walking out in front of the audience.

- Find images of old circus posters on the Internet and discuss their style. Get pupils to design a poster advertising Monsieur Mercury's trapeze stunt, focusing on their use of persuasive language.

- Split the class into groups and ask them to research the history of the circus. Make a class display of the similarities and differences between Victorian circuses and modern-day circuses.

- Circuses and zoos have been criticised in the past for their treatment of animals. Hold a class debate about the advantages and disadvantages of keeping animals in captivity.

- Set pupils some maths problems associated with ticket prices. For example, for one evening performance, 120 seats are filled, and tickets cost £7 each. How much does Mr Chipchase make? Mr Chipchase wants to make £700. Each seat is worth £15, how many seats does he have to fill?

- Explain that the danger of performers falling off their apparatus often draws a bigger audience to circuses. Explain that gravity makes things fall to the earth, and demonstrate it by getting pupils to drop a variety of objects, noting that some fall at different speeds. Split the class into groups and challenge them to make an object that will drop slowly. The group whose object takes the longest to hit the ground wins.

Reign of the Sea Dragons

Question Book:
Year 4, pages 22-23

Author / Source:
Sneed Collard

Genre:
Non-fiction — reference text

Cross-curricular links:
• Science (adaptation; food webs)

• Maths (conversion; scale)

Introduction

Sneed Collard is an American science writer. He has written many books for young people, many of which are non-fiction science texts. He developed an interest in science from an early age, as a result of both of his parents being biologists, and he aims to make his books interesting and accessible for younger audiences. *Reign of the Sea Dragons* is about the unusual creatures which lived in our oceans millions of years ago.

Answers

1. E.g. They show the reader how to pronounce the word that comes before the brackets.

2. E.g. To make something move forwards.

3. E.g. The elasmosaur had a long neck which let it sneak up on prey. The pliosaur had huge jaws and lots of teeth which helped it attack and kill large prey.

4. squid

5. The pliosaur eats the elasmosaur, which eats the squid.

6. the elasmosaur

7. E.g. To give the reader something to compare its teeth to so that they know how sharp they were.

8. E.g. They don't exist any more and are so different from animals which live in our oceans today that they seem like fantasy creatures. They are also very big and dangerous, just like dragons.

Extra Activities

• Ask pupils to write a short fantasy story in which they make the shocking discovery that creatures such as the elasmosaur and pliosaur are not actually extinct.

• Get pupils to invent their own sea creature. Ask them to draw a picture of their creature and write a short passage describing what it looks like, where it lives, what it eats, and how it goes about getting its food.

• Split the class into groups and assign each group an elasmosaur, pliosaur, ichthyosaur or mosasaur. Give them a large piece of paper with a picture of their creature in the middle, and then ask them to research how the creature is adapted to its environment and annotate the picture with their findings.

• With the class, discuss the food web mentioned in the extract. Explain the difference between a food web and a food chain. As a class, come up with some food chains, and then try to create a food web.

• The extract says the elasmosaur had a fifteen-foot neck, and the pliosaur was thirty feet long, with seven-foot jaws. Using calculators and the conversion of 1 foot = 0.3048 metres, get pupils to calculate these lengths in metres. Then take the class outside and measure the lengths in the playground so that they can visualise the size of the creatures. Back in the classroom, get pupils to draw scaled-down diagrams of the creatures, making sure to add a scale next to their drawing.

Peter Pan

Question Book:
Year 4, pages 24-25

Author / Source:
J.M. Barrie

Genre:
Classic fiction — novel extract

Cross-curricular links:
- Drama (playscript)
- PSHE (growing up)

Introduction

Peter Pan, J.M. Barrie's classic tale of the boy who never grew up, was originally written as a play. In 1911, it was republished as a novel under the title *Peter and Wendy*. It describes the adventures of the three Darling siblings, who are enticed by Peter Pan to travel with him to his home on the magical island of Neverland. Pupils may be familiar with the story, but before they read the extract, it may be helpful to give a brief outline of the plot and explain that Mr and Mrs Darling are the children's parents, and Nana is their dog.

Answers

1. E.g. He lets go of what he is holding and starts to fly.

2. E.g. Peter is better at flying — the author says he is more "elegant" than the other children, and that he was helping Wendy to start off with.

3. "Heavenly"

4. E.g. She might be worried about what would happen to them if they went outside.

5. He talks about mermaids and pirates.

6. E.g. Worried and confused because they can see the shadows of their three children, as well as someone else, flying around the nursery.

7. Any appropriate answer. E.g. I want to grow up, because when you grow up you can be independent, and you can do things like drive a car. OR E.g. I would like to be a child forever, because when you're a child you don't have to worry about things like having a job and paying bills.

Extra Activities

- With the whole class, discuss Barrie's writing style. For example, you could highlight the extensive use of direct speech and explore how it affects the pace of the extract.

- Make sure pupils are aware that in the novel, the Darling siblings fly with Peter Pan to the magical island of Neverland. Ask pupils to write and illustrate a postcard from one of the siblings to Mr and Mrs Darling, describing their journey to Neverland and what the island is like.

- Ask pupils to imagine that they wake up one morning to find they can fly. How might they feel? What would they do? Where would they go? Get them to write a short story based around this scenario.

- Explain that *Peter Pan* was originally written as a play. Working in groups, ask pupils to re-write the extract in the form of a playscript and then perform their scene for the class.

- Drawing on pupils' answers to question 7 in the Question Book, hold a class debate about the pros and cons of growing up. Ask half the class to argue that being a child is better, while the other half argue that being an adult is preferable.

Bletchley Park Codebreakers

Question Book:
Year 4, pages 26-27

Author / Source:
www.telegraph.co.uk

Genre:
Non-fiction — news article

Cross-curricular links:
* History (World War Two)
* Maths (cyphers; sequences)

Introduction

This extract is about the role a newspaper crossword played in recruiting people to work at Bletchley Park during World War Two. Bletchley is a mansion house in Buckinghamshire where the UK's Government Code and Cypher School (GC&CS) was based during the war, deciphering German codes. This work was vital to the war effort, and it has been estimated that it helped shorten the war by two to four years.

Answers

1. It is written in bold. E.g. Because it is the introduction, so it needs to stand out from the rest of the article.

2. To challenge people to prove that they could complete *The Daily Telegraph's* crossword in a few minutes.

3. They were interested in the winners because if they were so good at crosswords, they might be good codebreakers too.

4. E.g. Secret; classified; private. Because the government wanted as few people as possible to know what was happening at Bletchley Park so that the Germans would not find out that they were trying to break Germany's codes.

5. E.g. For both, you have to work out how your opponent thinks.

6. E.g. It helped the government to find people who were able to successfully break the German codes.

7. Any appropriate answer. E.g. I think I would have felt shocked that I had been chosen, and nervous because it would be a great responsibility. However, I would feel honoured to be serving my country.

Extra Activities

*   Get pupils to write a diary entry as Stanley Sedgewick, focusing on why he entered the competition and how he felt when he received the letter asking him to make an appointment to see Col Nichols.

*   Bletchley Park is now a museum. As a class, find out more about Bletchley Park using the Internet. Ask pupils to create a tourist leaflet for the museum, including some information about its history, as well as practical information for visitors. They should think about the layout of the leaflet and use of pictures.

*   Show pupils images of enigma machines and briefly explain how they work. Discuss the importance of the work at Bletchley, and with the class, create a timeline of the important events which Bletchley was involved in, such as the D-Day landings.

*   Explain that three-quarters of the workforce at Bletchley Park were women. In groups, get pupils to research the role of women during World War Two and to present their findings to the rest of the class.

*   Show pupils a cypher in which each letter of the alphabet is shifted four letters to the right, so A = E, B = F, etc. Get pupils to use the cypher to write encoded messages for their classmates to decrypt.

*   Explain the importance of mathematics in codebreaking. Give the class sequences of numbers with different rules and ask them to work out the rule to find the next number in each sequence.

Poems about Witches

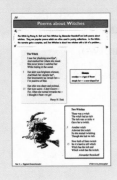

Question Book:
Year 4, pages 28-29

Author / Source:
Percy H. Ilott
Alexander Resnikoff

Genre:
Poetry

Cross-curricular links:
*   Art (illustration)
*   History (superstitions)

Introduction

The Witch by Percy H. Ilott and *Two Witches* by Alexander Resnikoff are two short poems that focus on similar topics but have different forms. They are both made up of three four-line stanzas, but they have different rhyme schemes, and *Two Witches* is a tongue twister that uses word play. Before reading *The Witch*, it may be useful to explain that cowslips are often associated with magic.

Answers

1. Any appropriate answer. E.g. To put in a potion.

2. c. red

3. E.g. He doesn't want her to know he's there because he's scared of what she might do.

4. Because they're both twitching — one because she's itching and one just because she likes to twitch.

5. a. E.g. The repetition of 'witch', 'which', 'itch' and 'twitch', which all contain similar sounds, makes the poem difficult to read out loud.
    b. 'which' and 'witch'.

6. E.g. The witch in the first poem seems scary, with a "sharp and pointed" chin, so the narrator leaves when she looks at him. In the second poem, the witches seem much funnier.

7. Any appropriate answer. E.g. I prefer *Two Witches* because it's fun to read out loud, and I think the idea of the two witches twitching is very funny. OR E.g. I prefer *The Witch* because I like the way the poet describes the witch so that I can imagine myself hiding in the wood watching her.

Extra Activities

*   Introduce the term 'homophone' — words which sound the same but are spelt differently and have different meanings, like 'witch' and 'which'. As a class, come up with a list of words which sound the same but have different meanings and spellings.

*   Ask pupils to write their own poem about a witch or witches, following the same rhyme scheme as one of the two poems. They could be encouraged to experiment with word play or tongue twisters.

*   Drawing on pupils' answers to question 7 in the Question Book, split the class into pairs and get them to discuss with their partner their favourite poem and the reasons why they prefer it.

*   Ask pupils to imagine that these two poems are being put into a poetry anthology and that they have been asked to provide the illustrations for one of the poems.

*   Explain that many people in Britain in the Middle Ages believed in witchcraft and superstitions. As a class, discuss examples of superstitions, such as the belief that the number 13 is unlucky and that you shouldn't walk under ladders. Ask the pupils what they think of superstitions and whether they are superstitious or not, e.g. do they own any 'lucky' objects or do certain things to avoid bad luck?

Swim, Bike, Run: Our Triathlon Story

Question Book:
Year 4, pages 30-31

Author / Source:
Alistair and Jonathan Brownlee

Genre:
Non-fiction — autobiography

Cross-curricular links:
- PSHE (role models)
- Geography (UK towns and cities)

Introduction

Alistair and Jonathan Brownlee are two of Britain's most successful triathletes, having achieved a number of Olympic, World, European and Commonwealth titles between them. Their autobiography is about their journey from growing up in Yorkshire, to becoming professional triathletes and competing at the 2012 London Olympics, where they won gold and bronze respectively. The book describes their relationship as brothers, as well as their development as sportsmen. Before reading the extract with the class, make sure that pupils understand what a triathlon involves, and explain that the 'transition area' is the place where triathletes change between the swimming, cycling and running legs of the race.

Answers

1. "the biggest two hours of your life"

2. E.g. Because he usually sleeps badly before an important race, and two nights earlier he had been unable to sleep, so he thought that his nerves would keep him awake.

3. E.g. He felt excited. This is different to how he usually feels before a race — usually he feels nervous.

4. E.g. To emphasise how loud and sudden the noise of the crowd was.

5. E.g. Because he saw how many people were there to support them, and this helped him to relax.

6. E.g. It is written in the first person. OR E.g. It describes the authors' feelings about important events in their lives.

7. Any appropriate answer. E.g. I think I would feel excited to be representing my country. I would also feel nervous because I would want to do well in the competition.

Extra Activities

- As a class, explore the features of autobiographies. How is this autobiography different from a standard autobiography? Discuss how the book alternates between the brothers' voices and the effect this has.

- Ask pupils to write an autobiographical passage about a recent school event, such as sports day or a school trip. Working in pairs, get pupils to compare what they have written. What are the similarities and differences between their perspectives on the same event?

- Discuss why the Brownlee brothers are inspirational figures. Ask pupils to make a poster about someone who inspires them. They should include a picture of their inspirational figure and a short passage about who the figure is and why they find them inspiring.

- Explain to the class that every British athlete who won a gold medal at the 2012 London Olympics and Paralympics had a post box painted gold in their honour. Most of the post boxes are located in or near the athletes' home towns. Alistair Brownlee's post box is in Horsforth, West Yorkshire. Give pupils a map of the UK and ask them to find Horsforth. Challenge pupils to find the location of other gold post boxes.

Chris Hoy (Edinburgh),
Ellie Simmonds (Swansea),
Jessica Ennis-Hill (Sheffield)

The Word Party

Question Book:
Year 5, pages 2-3

Author / Source:
Richard Edwards

Genre:
Poetry

Cross-curricular links:

* Drama (mime)

* Art (illustrating imagery)

Introduction

Richard Edwards is a successful children's writer. As well as writing collections of poetry for children, he has also written several popular picture books. His writing is original, imaginative and entertaining. In this poem, Edwards takes a comical look at what happens inside the dictionary. His imaginative use of personification will encourage pupils to look at words in a new light and explore creative ways of using figurative language in their writing.

Answers

1. sniffing and picking your nose

2. E.g. Angry, because people often use swear words when they're angry.

3. E.g. Because they are joined together with a hyphen.

4. E.g. To make it stand out and make the ending of the poem seem very sudden and unexpected.

5. b. personification

6. Any appropriate answer. E.g. Line 12 is my favourite because code words are linked to spies, so the idea of code words carrying "secret folders" as if they were spies is clever and funny.

7. Any appropriate answer. E.g. Interesting, because it makes you imagine that all the words in the dictionary have different personalities and that they're all having a party inside the dictionary.

Extra Activities

* As a class, discuss the rhyme scheme and rhythm of the poem. Get pupils to identify the rhyme scheme and then compare the number of syllables in the pairs of lines that rhyme. Why do they have the same number of syllables? How would it affect the rhythm of the poem if they were different?

* Ask pupils to learn the poem by heart and then recite it in front of the class.

* Suggest some other adjectives (e.g. rushed, gentle, worried) and ask pupils to come up with their own phrases to describe how such words might behave at a party. Pupils could then write their own "Word Party" poem, making sure that their rhyming couplets have the same number of syllables in each line.

* Challenge pupils to think of one synonym and one antonym for each of the adjectives used in the poem to describe a type of word.

  complicated
   — difficult / easy
  silly
   — daft / sensible
  small
   — tiny / huge

* Secretly assign each pupil a line from the poem and ask them to think of a mime for their line. Pupils should then take it in turns to perform their mime while the rest of the class tries to guess which line they have been assigned.

* Ask pupils to draw or paint a picture to illustrate the line of the poem they were assigned in the previous activity. The pupils' pictures could be used to create a class display of *The Word Party*.

An Astronaut's Guide to Life on Earth

Question Book:
Year 5, pages 4-5

Author / Source:
Chris Hadfield

Genre:
Non-fiction — memoir

Cross-curricular links:

*   PSHE (ambitions)

*   Science (the solar system)

*   D&T (building a sundial)

Introduction

Chris Hadfield grew up on a farm in southern Ontario, Canada. He served as an engineer and fighter pilot in the Royal Canadian Air Force but, after watching the Apollo 11 moon landing, aspired to be an astronaut. In 1995, he achieved this goal when he undertook his first space shuttle mission. While commanding the International Space Station in 2013, Chris built up a large audience on social media with his tweets, photographs and videos from space. Before pupils read this extract, show them a video of Space Shuttle *Atlantis* taking off in 1995.

Answers

1. E.g. gets stronger; grows; increases

2. E.g. Because leaving the planet is a very important event in his life. By putting this sentence on a separate line, he makes it stand out and emphasises how important it is to him.

3. Any appropriate answer. E.g. I am a bit surprised because the spacecraft sounds very uncomfortable. However, being in the spacecraft means that Chris is about to go into space, which is something he wants to do, so it's not that surprising that he's happy to be there.

4. a. bends, lurches, twangs b. E.g. Because they show that the spacecraft was moving violently and awkwardly, so they add to the idea that the journey will be uncomfortable.

5. E.g. They create a vivid picture in the reader's mind of the violence of take-off and how it feels to travel in a spacecraft. They also describe Chris's excitement as the vehicle takes off, which makes the reader feel excited about what will happen next, and about the idea of going into space.

Extra Activities

*   Drawing on pupils' answers to questions 4 and 5 in the Question Book, discuss the description of the take-off in lines 21-25 of the text. Highlight Chris's choice of vocabulary and ask pupils to identify words that help to emphasise the power and drama of the take-off. Challenge pupils to suggest alternative words and phrases that would create a similar effect.

*   Show pupils the video of Space Shuttle *Atlantis* taking off again, and then ask them to write a description of the take-off from the perspective of an external observer. Encourage them to think about their choice of vocabulary and to use figurative language. As a class, compare the pupils' descriptions with Chris Hadfield's, and discuss the difference between witnessing an event and experiencing it first-hand.

*   Chris Hadfield began working towards his goal of becoming an astronaut at a young age. Ask pupils to think of something they would like to achieve as an adult. They should write a letter to their future selves, describing what they hope to be doing and how they will work towards achieving this ambition.

*   Using a torch to represent the Sun and a globe for the Earth, explain how the rotation of the Earth causes night and day, and creates the impression of the Sun moving across the sky from east to west. Pupils could then apply this knowledge by constructing a sundial, using a metre stick for the shaft and making chalk marks on the ground to record the position of its shadow at different times of day.

Why Recycle?

Question Book:
Year 5, pages 6-7

Author / Source:
www.thinkcans.net

Genre:
Non-fiction — persuasive text

Cross-curricular links:
- PSHE (recycling)
- Science (pollution)
- Maths (statistics)

Introduction

In the last 15 years, levels of recycling in the UK have increased significantly, but the average UK household still recycles less than 50% of its waste. Waste that isn't recycled is either sent to landfill or incinerated, both of which have serious environmental consequences. This text explains how waste damages the environment and how recycling can help to reduce levels of waste. Before pupils read the text, ask them whether they think recycling is important and what they recycle at home and at school.

Answers

1. E.g. Because it wastes natural resources, and it damages the environment.

2. It is buried in landfill sites or burned.

3. E.g. Everyone should try to live in a way that uses as few natural resources as possible so that there are enough left for people in the future.

4. E.g. When something is recycled, it's broken down and turned into new products, but when something is reused, it's used again as it is.

5. Any appropriate answer. E.g. Yes, because it lists the most important points in the article, which helps you to remember them.

6. E.g. To persuade people to recycle more.

7. E.g. It makes the text seem more personal, so the reader is more likely to be persuaded by the text because they feel like they are involved in doing the things it describes.

Extra Activities

- Ask pupils to explain whether reading the text has affected their views on recycling. If they didn't think recycling was important, has reading the text changed their view? Why / why not? If they already regarded recycling as important, has the text given them a better understanding of why it matters?

- Discuss pupils' answers to questions 5-7 in the Question Book. How do techniques like the summary and the use of the first person plural help to achieve the purpose of the text? What other techniques has the writer used to make the text informative and persuasive? Can pupils think of any ways to improve the language or layout of the text to make it more informative and persuasive?

- Ask pupils to research the ecological impact of waste plastic, including the accumulation of plastic in oceans (e.g. the great Pacific garbage patch) and its impact on marine wildlife. Pupils should use their research to create a poster that will inform people about the ecological damage caused by plastic and persuade them to reduce the amount of plastic they use.

- Get pupils to weigh the waste and recycling produced by their class and other classes every day for a week, and calculate a daily average for each class. They can then use their findings to draw bar graphs showing which class produces the most waste and which does the most recycling.

Tales of King Arthur

Question Book:
Year 5, pages 8-9

Author / Source:
Felicity Brooks

Genre:
Fiction — legend

Cross-curricular links:
*   History (reliability of sources)

Introduction

King Arthur is said to have lived around the year 500, but the first detailed narrative account of his life was not written until the 1130s, by the Welsh monk, Geoffrey of Monmouth. As a result, Arthur is a much-debated figure in British history, and historians are still uncertain whether or not the Arthurian legends have any basis in fact. This modern retelling of one of the best-known Arthurian legends is written in an engaging and approachable style. As pupils read the extract, focus their attention on the author's use of direct speech to drive the action.

Answers

1. E.g. Because he wanted people to think that he was the "trueborn king".

2. E.g. No. Ector made Kay go to the stone with him and try to put the sword back in. This shows that Ector didn't believe Kay and wanted him to prove that he had pulled the sword out himself.

3. E.g. Because his father knew that he had lied about pulling the sword out of the stone. He was embarrassed that his father had found out, and maybe worried that his father would be angry with him.

4. E.g. He uses one long sentence with lots of commas in it, which shows that Arthur is talking quickly. He also uses "..." and repeats the phrase "and I", which shows that Arthur is stuttering and repeating himself.

5. "The blade slid back in, like a warm knife into butter."

6. Any appropriate answer. E.g. I think he felt confused and surprised. He may also have felt excited about the idea of being king and nervous about how difficult it might be.

Extra Activities

*   As a class, discuss the effect that the extensive use of direct speech in this extract has on the reader.

*   Drawing on their answers to question 6 in the Question Book, ask pupils to imagine how Arthur reacted to the news that he was king. Pupils should write a continuation of the extract, describing Arthur's response. They should use direct speech as much as possible.

*   Kay is an ambivalent figure in this extract. Ask pupils to think about his relationship with Arthur and to write a diary entry from his point of view, exploring his attitude to the events described in the extract.

*   Get pupils to use the information in the extract as the basis for a newspaper article about the discovery of Britain's "trueborn king". Make sure they use appropriate language and presentational features.

*   Ask pupils to identify the features of the extract which suggest it is a legend. Can they think of any other features of legends? As a class, discuss the reliability of legends as historical sources. Why might historians regard legends as unreliable? Do legends contain any useful information about the past?

*   Explain that legends are often exaggerated accounts of ordinary events. Ask pupils to write a short, factual passage describing their journey to school and then rewrite the passage in the form of a legend. Encourage pupils to think about which passage would be more reliable as a historical source.

The Great Fire of London

Question Book:
Year 5, pages 10-11

Author / Source:
George Szirtes

Genre:
Poetry

Cross-curricular links:

- History (the Great Fire of London)

- Geography (using maps)

Introduction

The Great Fire of London started just after midnight on 2nd September 1666 in Thomas Farynor's bakery on Pudding Lane. Because of overcrowding and the use of flammable building materials, such as wood and straw, the fire quickly spread throughout much of the City of London. By the time it was extinguished on 5th September, the fire had destroyed thousands of buildings and made an estimated 100,000 people homeless. This poem, by the Hungarian-born poet and translator George Szirtes, uses the extended metaphor of "firebirds" to offer an original perspective on this dramatic event. As pupils read the poem, encourage them to think about the various poetic techniques Szirtes uses to create a vivid image of the fire.

Answers

1. E.g. The fire was started by the embers of Thomas Farynor's oven.

2. E.g. It tells you that the fire was very hot, because it was making whole barrels of water boil.

3. "Like robins who had never sung a note"

4. It means that the bridge was on fire.

5. b. a metaphor

6. Negative: the fire destroyed "whole districts" of the city. Positive: the fire got rid of the plague.

7. c. ABAB

8. Any appropriate answer. E.g. Yes, because it brings the fire to life and helps you to imagine how it might have looked and sounded. For example, the idea of the fire being like birds helps you to picture how the sparks flew through the air and how the flames moved from roof to roof.

Extra Activities

- Give pupils a list of techniques that are used in the poem (e.g. personification, metaphor, simile, onomatopoeia) and challenge them to identify at least one example of each. As a class, discuss the effect that these techniques have on the reader.

- Ask pupils to write their own narrative poem about a historical event that they have recently studied. Make sure they include some key facts about the event in their poem, and encourage them to use an extended metaphor, similar to Szirtes's "firebirds", to engage the reader and bring the event to life.

- Divide the class into groups and assign each group one day from 2nd to 5th September 1666. Ask each group to find out about how the Great Fire of London developed during their day and to prepare a TV news bulletin to present to the class. The news bulletins should describe the key events that occurred on each day, and could also include imagined interviews with eyewitnesses.

- Give pupils a map of the City of London and challenge them to find some of the key locations associated with the Great Fire, such as Pudding Lane, Fish Street, London Bridge, St Paul's Cathedral and the Monument to the Great Fire of London. Ask them to write down the grid reference for each location.

The Iron Man

Question Book:
Year 5, pages 12-13

Author / Source:
Ted Hughes

Genre:
Fiction — novel extract

Cross-curricular links:

* Science (properties of materials)

* Maths (nets)

Introduction

Ted Hughes (1930-1998) is widely regarded as one of the greatest English poets of the twentieth century. He was also a popular children's author, and *The Iron Man* is one of his most successful works for children. Like so much of Hughes's writing, *The Iron Man* is written in a vivid and engaging style, and this extract gives pupils the chance to explore techniques that engage the reader, including figurative and descriptive language, variations in sentence length and the use of questions. As pupils read the extract, focus their attention on the way Hughes uses language to make them want to keep reading.

Answers

1. E.g. edge; tip; verge

2. E.g. They help the reader to imagine what the Iron Man looked like because they compare different parts of him to familiar things like "a dustbin" and "headlamps".

3. Any appropriate answer. E.g. He had never seen the sea before, so maybe he didn't understand what it was and he didn't realise that it would be dangerous to step off the cliff towards the sea.

4. E.g. To show the reader that the Iron Man is bouncing down the cliff, hitting lots of things on the way, and to help the reader imagine the noise he makes as he falls.

5. "the sea, chewing away at the edge of the rocky beach"

6. Any appropriate answer. E.g. Yes, because in this extract, it seems like the Iron Man has been destroyed, so I want to read more of the novel to find out whether he manages to survive falling off the cliff.

Extra Activities

* Ask pupils to annotate their copy of the extract, underlining words and phrases that engage the reader, and labelling examples of similes, personification, onomatopoeia, repetition, etc. As a class, discuss the words, phrases and literary techniques that pupils have identified, and explore their effect on the reader.

* This extract is taken from the beginning of *The Iron Man*. Ask pupils to write a few paragraphs describing what they think happens next. Encourage them to write in the same style as the extract, using as many of the same techniques as they can.

* In this extract, Hughes captures the reader's attention and sets the scene in just ten lines. Challenge pupils to write their own ten-line opening to a short story about a mysterious creature, which engages the reader and creates an atmospheric setting.

* Ask pupils to find out about the properties of iron and to suggest some advantages and disadvantages of being made of iron. Ask pupils to research the properties of some other materials (e.g. salt, wood, paper, plastic) and explain which they think would be most suitable to make an animate giant from.

* Get pupils to design and build an 'Iron Man' consisting entirely of regular cuboids. They should draw a net of each cuboid on thin cardboard, then cut it out and fold it into shape. Encourage pupils to make careful measurements when drawing their nets.

Pompeii

Question Book:
Year 5, pages 14-15

Author / Source:
Catherine Heygate

Genre:
Non-fiction — reference text

Cross-curricular links:
- History (the Roman Empire)
- Geography (volcanoes)
- Art (mosaics)

Introduction

In the first century AD, Pompeii was a thriving Roman city. However, the devastating eruption of Mount Vesuvius in 79 AD destroyed the city, killing its inhabitants and burying the site under several metres of volcanic ash. In the mid-eighteenth century, archaeologists began excavating Pompeii and found that much of the city had been extraordinarily well preserved by the layers of ash covering it. As a result, Pompeii is now one of our most important sources of information about life in the Roman Empire. Before pupils read the text, make sure they understand what a volcano is.

Answers

1. E.g. To carry water into a city.

2. E.g. People in Roman cities had running water in their homes like many people do today, and they went to the theatre for entertainment like some people do.

3. E.g. Because Pliny the Younger wrote about it.

4. E.g. They weren't worried about them. Earthquakes were common in the area, and they didn't know that they were a sign that the volcano was going to erupt.

5. E.g. Because the city was preserved by the rock and ash from the volcano, so we can find out about life in the Roman Empire by studying all the things that have survived.

6. Any appropriate answer. E.g. Yes, because they break the text up into shorter sections, and they tell you what each section is about, so they make the text easier to read and understand.

Extra Activities

- The last question in the Question Book asks pupils to comment on the layout of the text. As a class, discuss pupils' answers to this question, and ask them to suggest additional features that would make the text easier to understand (e.g. illustrations, underlining, a glossary).

- Ask pupils to find out more about the aspects of Roman life mentioned in the first section of the text. They should use their research to write an informative text about life in the Roman Empire, using the presentational features identified in the class discussion to ensure that their text is easy to understand.

- Using the information in the text and their own research, ask pupils to write a newspaper article reporting the eruption of Mount Vesuvius in 79 AD.

- Explain the difference between active, dormant and extinct volcanoes. Assign pupils volcanoes from around the world to research (e.g. Arthur's Seat, Krakatoa, Novarupta). Pupils should use their research to create a fact sheet with key information about their volcano, including a map of its location, whether it is active, dormant or extinct and the date of its most recent eruption (if known).

- Roman buildings were often decorated with mosaics, many examples of which are preserved in Pompeii. Show pupils some pictures of Roman mosaics, and then ask them to design and make their own, using coloured paper or cardboard to make their tiles.

From a Railway Carriage

Question Book:
Year 5, pages 16-17

Author / Source:
Robert Louis Stevenson

Genre:
Classic poetry

Cross-curricular links:
*   History (Victorian railways)
*   Maths (timetables)

Introduction

Robert Louis Stevenson (1850-1894) was a Scottish writer and poet. This poem, which describes a journey on a steam train, was published in 1885. The first fully steam-powered railway in the world, the Liverpool and Manchester Railway, had opened in 1830, and by the 1880s, Britain had several thousand miles of railway lines. The rise of the railways transformed long-distance travel in the UK, and this poem reflects the Victorians' fascination with train travel. Read the poem out loud with the class, focusing on the effect created by its rhythm.

Answers

1. E.g. Because comparing the speed of the train to these creatures makes the train seem magical too. OR E.g. Because fairies and witches can fly and the train is going so fast that it feels like it's flying too.

2. "horses and cattle"

3. b. a simile

4. E.g. The things he can see through the train window.

5. E.g. Because you just see these things quickly through the train window, and then they disappear from sight, so you'll probably never see them again.

6. E.g. The rhythm of the poem is like the rhythm of the train, so it helps the reader to imagine what it's like to travel on the train.

7. Any appropriate answer. E.g. Yes, because it describes lots of different things, one after the other. This helps you imagine the way different views flash past the window when you're on a train.

Extra Activities

*   Explore how Stevenson creates the train-like rhythm of the poem. As a class, annotate the poem, underlining the stressed syllables in each line, then read the poem aloud again, with everyone tapping out the pattern of stressed and unstressed syllables on their tables.

*   Suggest some other modes of transport that have a distinctive rhythm (e.g. marching, horse riding) and discuss the pattern of syllables that would mirror their rhythm. Get pupils to write some rhyming couplets for each mode of transport, focusing on using stressed and unstressed syllables to recreate their rhythms.

*   Get pupils to write a poem describing a memorable journey that they have undertaken.

*   Ask pupils to find out about how people and goods were transported before the invention of the railways (e.g. canals, horses). What were the disadvantages of these modes of transport? How did the introduction of rail travel change things? Pupils should use their research to create a promotional leaflet for a Victorian railway company, explaining the advantages of rail travel over other forms of transport.

*   Get pupils to find train timetables for the station nearest to school. Challenge pupils to use the timetables to plan a journey that will take them as far as possible from the starting station within four hours.

Tracking Basking Sharks

Question Book:
Year 5, pages 18-19

Author / Source:
www.independent.co.uk

Genre:
Non-fiction — news article

Cross-curricular links:

- Science (marine organisms)

- Art (drawing activity)

Introduction

Basking sharks are huge fish — the largest recorded specimen was more than 12 m long. As filter feeders, they use their exceptionally large mouths and specially-adapted gills to filter plankton from seawater. This article describes a project which aims to find out more about basking sharks by tagging them with GPS devices and tracking their movements. Before reading the article with the class, show pupils some pictures of basking sharks and explain how they are adapted to feed on plankton.

Answers

1. E.g. Because basking sharks eat plankton, and the plankton in British waters is attracting them to areas where scientists can study them.

2. E.g. Sharks will be fitted with tracking devices, which will calculate their location every time they come to the surface.

3. E.g. difficult to find

4. E.g. She thinks they're really interesting because they're huge but also very mysterious.

5. "ready to leap into action"

6. E.g. Because scientists wouldn't have had the right technology, like satellites or GPS, 100 years ago.

7. Any appropriate answer. E.g. I think it's a good idea because basking sharks are endangered and tracking them might help scientists to protect them. Also, we don't know much about the sharks, so it's a good idea to find out more about them by tracking them.

Extra Activities

- Get pupils to briefly summarise the information in the article by writing a few words under each of the following headings: 'who', 'what', 'where' and 'why'.

- As a class, discuss the presentation and language features of news articles and their effect on the reader. Emphasise the use of headlines in news articles to engage the reader's interest. Do pupils find the headline of this article engaging? Can they think of a better one? Show pupils some other news articles without their headlines and ask pupils to suggest headlines for them.

- Emphasise how little we know about the behaviour and life-cycle of basking sharks, and then ask pupils to write a short story from the perspective of a basking shark, imagining its secret life under the sea.

- Assign pupils different marine organisms that can be found around the British coast. Pupils should research their organism, then draw a picture of it and write a short passage describing it. The pupils' work could be used to create a classroom display about British sea life.

hermit crabs, curlews, herring gulls, otters, grey seals, kelp, marram grass

A Letter from E.B. White

Question Book:
Year 5, pages 20-21

Author / Source:
E.B. White

Genre:
Non-fiction — letter

Cross-curricular links:
*   Science (spiders)

Introduction

E.B. White's letter to his editor is full of subtle humour and gentle eccentricity. Some students may not have read *Charlotte's Web*, so make sure that all pupils read the introduction before they read the letter. Ensure that pupils are aware that, in the book, Charlotte is a spider and Wilbur is a pig, and both animals can talk. Before pupils read the letter, ask them to think of reasons why authors might write books.

Answers

1. E.g. A weakness can be used to describe something that can't be resisted. E.B. White says that animals are a weakness with him because he can't resist writing about animals or being fascinated by them.

2. E.g. When a person changes for the worse.

3. E.g. He thinks that adults teach children to dislike spiders.

4. E.g. Because it makes the spiders' webs sound beautiful and shows how skilful and hardworking spiders are.

5. c. metaphor

6. E.g. Kind and funny. He seems like a kind man because he treats the spiders in a gentle and caring way, and he sounds like he has a sense of humour because he says that "A book is a sneeze".

7. Any appropriate answer. E.g. Yes, because he says "A book is a sneeze", which tells you that he wrote the book because he felt like it was something he just had to do, rather than something he decided to do. OR E.g. No, I don't think it explains why he wrote the book — it just explains why he likes spiders.

Extra Activities

*   With the whole class, discuss what E.B. White means when he says "A book is a sneeze". How does this explanation compare with the reasons for writing that pupils suggested before reading the letter?

*   As a group, discuss the techniques E.B. White uses to describe spiders, and how they affect the reader.

*   Ask pupils to imagine that they are E.B. White. They should write a letter to their friend, using figurative language, to describe their favourite animal.

*   Get pupils to create a spidergram of all the adjectives, verbs and adverbs they can think of that describe the way spiders look and behave. Pupils should then write a short descriptive passage about a spider, using as many of these words as possible.

*   In the letter, E.B. White describes spiders as "skilful, amusing and useful". Ask pupils to research spiders' behaviour to find evidence for and against this view. They can then use the evidence they have gathered to debate positive and negative views of spiders.

*   The spider E.B. White describes in his letter is from the species *Araneus cavaticus*. Get pupils to research this species and produce a poster describing its appearance, habitat and behaviour.

Poems about Knights

Question Book:
Year 5, pages 22-23

Author / Source:
Hugh Chesterman
Sir Walter Scott

Genre:
Classic poetry

Cross-curricular links:
• Art (designing shields)

Introduction

Sir Nicketty Nox is one of many children's poems published in the early twentieth century by the English poet and writer Hugh Chesterman. *Lochinvar* by Sir Walter Scott is an eight-stanza poem, of which the first two stanzas are reproduced here. *Lochinvar* was first published in 1808 as part of Scott's much longer poem, *Marmion*. *Sir Nicketty Nox* and *Lochinvar* describe two very different fictional knights, giving pupils an opportunity to compare the characters of Sir Nicketty Nox and Lochinvar, as well as the different poetic techniques used by the two poets.

Answers

1. Any appropriate answer. E.g. Sir Nicketty Nox is old, but Lochinvar is young. Sir Nicketty Nox is married, but Lochinvar is not.

2. d. a simile

3. E.g. It suggests that he's shrivelled and wrinkly.

4. AABB

5. E.g. brave; fearless; daring; bold

6. E.g. Because he wanted to marry Ellen. When he didn't arrive in time, she married someone else.

7. Any appropriate answer. E.g. I would prefer to meet Lochinvar because he is loyal and brave, and the poem says there never was a knight like him. Nicketty Nox, on the other hand, sounds boring and grumpy.

Extra Activities

• As a class, compare the form of the two poems. Ask pupils to identify the rhyme scheme of *Sir Nicketty Nox* and compare it with that of *Lochinvar*. How many syllables are there in each line of *Lochinvar*? How does this compare with the number of syllables per line in *Sir Nicketty Nox*?

• In *Lochinvar*, Scott often uses unusual word order and old-fashioned language. Ask pupils to rewrite the poem in prose, using modern language and standard English grammar. Encourage them to use a dictionary to find out the meaning of any words they are unfamiliar with.

• Ask pupils to think about which of the two poems they prefer. They should write a review of their preferred poem, explaining why they like it and discussing any aspects of it that they don't like.

• Get pupils to invent their own knightly character. They should write and illustrate an acrostic poem based on their knight's name. Ask them to include some animal-based similes like those in line 3 of *Sir Nicketty Nox* to describe their knight's defining characteristics.

• Ask pupils to design shields for Sir Nicketty Nox and Lochinvar. Encourage them to think about how they can represent the knights' characters that are mentioned in the poems on their shields.

The Wind in the Willows (musical)

Question Book:
Year 5, pages 24-25

Author / Source:
Stephen Kingsbury and Ben Sleep

Genre:
Fiction — playscript

Cross-curricular links:
• Drama (role-play)
• PSHE (crime and the law)

Introduction

The Wind in the Willows by Kenneth Grahame, first published in 1908, is a popular children's novel. Set in the Thames Valley, it follows the adventures of Mole, Rat, Toad and Badger. Stephen Kingsbury and Ben Sleep have worked together to adapt well-known novels, such as *The Wind in the Willows*, into musicals which schools and other groups can perform. Read the extract through with the class, asking for volunteers to read a part each. You could also ask an additional pupil to read the stage directions aloud.

Answers

1. E.g. To show that the judge is shouting.

2. E.g. He has stolen a car, driven dangerously and behaved rudely towards a police officer.

3. E.g. They give extra information about what is happening on stage so that the reader knows which actors are present and what they're doing.

4. E.g. He thinks Toad should be dealt with strictly for his many serious crimes. He thinks that Toad is cunning but that he can deal with him.

5. E.g. He apologises and says he understands that his crimes are serious. He also tries to defend himself — he denies that what he did was stealing and claims he was joking when he was rude to the policeman.

6. E.g. Because he thinks the policeman is insulting him by calling him a toad.

7. E.g. He calls the policeman a "nincompoop", but wants to punish Toad for doing the same thing. He says Toad's actions are "unforgivable" as no one, whatever their rank, should be rude to a police officer.

Extra Activities

• Split the pupils into groups and ask them to prepare a performance of the extract. Ask the pupils to think about the emotions and attitudes of each character and how they should concentrate on using their voices and actions to express this.

• Divide the class into pairs, one playing the role of the policeman and the other playing Toad. Ask them to imagine the policeman is interrogating Toad to try and find out what happened. What questions will the policeman ask? How will Toad respond?

• Ask pupils to write a news article describing the events that led to Toad's trial. They should pay particular attention to the layout of their article, using a headline, quotations and pictures.

• Stealing cars, driving dangerously and being rude to police officers are serious offences in the real world. Discuss as a class what they think the consequences of this behaviour would be in today's society. What do they think the punishment should be for each of these offences? Which of these offences do they think is the worst, and why?

• Discuss as a class whether the pupils think it is fair for the judge to call Toad's behaviour towards the policeman "unforgivable". Is there such a thing as an unforgivable crime?

Hiding Out

Question Book:
Year 5, pages 26-27

Author / Source:
Elizabeth Laird

Genre:
Fiction — novel extract

Cross-curricular links:
- History (prehistoric Europe)
- Art (cave paintings)

Introduction

Elizabeth Laird is a prolific children's author. In a career spanning more than forty years, she has written over 150 novels and picture books for children. Her novel *Hiding Out* focuses on a boy called Peter who must find a way to survive when his parents accidentally leave him alone in the French countryside with no food, water or shelter, and no knowledge of the French language. This extract describes the moment when Peter's parents accidentally abandon him. As they read, encourage pupils to think about how the author creates tension and drama in the extract.

Answers

1. E.g. Because he doesn't want to leave the cave.

2. E.g. He didn't want to travel with his dad and Julian, so he waited for them to leave. He planned to get into his mum's car instead, but she left before he was able to.

3. E.g. By using exclamation marks.

4. E.g. It makes that part of the text seem very dramatic because the short sentences make it seem as if the events are happening very quickly.

5. a. E.g. dreadful; terrible; horrible; frightful
   b. E.g. Because the silence shows that Peter is all on his own, so it seems dreadful to him.

6. Any appropriate answer. E.g. I think I would feel frightened to be all on my own. I would also feel upset and angry that everyone had left without me.

Extra Activities

- As a class, discuss the techniques that the author uses in this extract to set the scene and create tension. Explore the effect of the contrast between longer sentences at the start of the extract and very short sentences in lines 18-21, the use of dramatic verbs ("shrieked", "racing") in lines 22-23, and the author's subtle use of adjectives and adverbs throughout the extract to set the scene and convey Peter's feelings.

- Ask pupils to write a short story in which something unexpected happens to the characters while they are on holiday. Encourage pupils to vary sentence length and vocabulary to create tension in their stories.

- Ask pupils to write Peter's internal dialogue, using the first person to describe his thoughts and feelings at different points in the extract.

- Explain that examples of prehistoric art have been found in caves in France and elsewhere in Europe. Show pupils some examples of European cave art and make sure pupils understand when they were produced. As a class, discuss why cave paintings are an important source for historians studying prehistoric Europe. What can they tell us about that period? Why might they be difficult to interpret?

- Charcoal and chalk were often used in prehistoric cave paintings. Get pupils to create their own cave drawings using these materials.

Wolves in the UK

Question Book:
Year 5, pages 28-29

Author / Source:
www.independent.co.uk

Genre:
Non-fiction — news article

Cross-curricular links:
- Science (wolves)
- Drama (scriptwriting)

Introduction

For many centuries, wolves were found throughout the British Isles, but between the fifteenth and eighteenth centuries, a combination of hunting and deforestation gradually caused them to disappear from the UK. As part of the 'rewilding' movement, prominent figures like Chris Packham and David Attenborough have recently begun to call for large predators such as wolves to be reintroduced to parts of Britain, arguing that they would help to rebalance British ecosystems. Before reading the article with the class, ask pupils to suggest adjectives that they would use to describe wolves.

Answers

1. E.g. It suggests that he really wants wolves to be reintroduced and that he is working really hard to persuade people that this is a good idea.

2. none

3. E.g. He means that people need to understand that wolves aren't that dangerous to humans and that they're important for the environment.

4. Scotland

5. E.g. Because people would pay money to see them.

6. E.g. Because there haven't been any wolves in the UK for a long time, and people are scared of them.

7. Any appropriate answer. E.g. Yes, because I think it would be exciting to see a wolf in the wild, and the article says that it would be good for the community and the environment. OR E.g. No, because I think wolves are frightening, and it wouldn't be safe to do things like camping if there were wolves in the UK.

Extra Activities

- With the whole class, discuss the adjectives pupils listed before reading the article. What adjectives do they think Chris Packham would use to describe wolves? Is his view of wolves similar or different to theirs?

- As a class, discuss the depiction of wolves in popular culture. Can pupils think of any fairy tales, nursery rhymes or other stories about wolves? Do they present wolves in a positive or negative light? How might these stories affect people's attitudes towards wolves?

- Ask pupils to write their own fairy tale which presents wolves in a positive light.

- Get pupils to research grey wolves and design an illustrated fact sheet describing their habitat, diet and behaviour. Drawing on the pupils' research, you could then hold a class debate about whether wolves should be reintroduced into the UK and why they would be best suited to reintroduction in Scotland.

- Working in groups, ask pupils to devise a marketing campaign to persuade people to support the reintroduction of wolves in the UK. They will need to think of a slogan and logo for their campaign, design a poster and write a script for a short TV advertisement promoting wolves. Make sure pupils focus on making their campaign as persuasive as possible.

The Wolves of Willoughby Chase

Question Book:
Year 5, pages 30-31

Author / Source:
Joan Aiken

Genre:
Classic fiction — novel extract

Cross-curricular links:
*   Art (cartoon strip)

Introduction

The British author Joan Aiken (1924-2004) received many awards for her work, including an MBE for her services to children's literature. *The Wolves of Willoughby Chase* is the first in a series of twelve novels. Set in a fictionalised version of nineteenth-century England that is terrorised by marauding wolves, the novel follows Bonnie and her orphaned cousin, Sylvia, as they struggle to escape the clutches of their unscrupulous guardian, Miss Slighcarp. Before pupils read the extract, ask them to explain what suspense is.

Answers

1. third

2. "wasted precious moments"

3. E.g. She feels upset and frightened because she thinks it would be safer to go back to the house, and she doesn't understand where Bonnie is taking her.

4. E.g. It makes you worried that Bonnie and Sylvia won't be able to find anyone to help them.

5. E.g. They are the wolves in the distance that are chasing Bonnie and Sylvia.

6. Any appropriate answer. E.g. I think she feels glad to see him because he might be able to protect them from the wolves. She also feels confused because she doesn't know who he is or where he came from.

7. E.g. Bonnie is in control. You can tell because she is confident and knows her way around and decides where to go, while Sylvia just follows her.

Extra Activities

*   As a class, explore the techniques Aiken uses to create tension and suspense in this extract. How does the setting contribute to the tense atmosphere? Why are the wolves important? How does Bonnie's behaviour help to build suspense? Why is it important that Sylvia doesn't know where they are going?

*   Give pupils a visual prompt, such as a picture of a darkened house or an overgrown garden, and ask them to write a short story inspired by it. Pupils should focus on creating tension and suspense in their stories.

*   Divide the class into two groups. Ask pupils from the first group to write a diary entry describing the events in the extract from Bonnie's perspective, while those in the second group write a diary entry from Sylvia's viewpoint. As a class, compare the two groups' diary entries. What do the similarities and differences between them suggest about the way different people may view the same events?

*   Ask pupils to create a cartoon strip of the extract. Encourage them to think about how they can convey the tense atmosphere of the text in their drawings.

*   Thinking back to the news article about the reintroduction of wolves to the UK (p.28-29 in the Year 5 Question Book; p.57 in the Teacher Book), discuss whether the extract from *The Wolves of Willoughby Chase* gives an accurate portrayal of what might happen if wolves were reintroduced. How might reading this extract affect people's attitudes towards the reintroduction of wolves?

An Interview with Nixie Labs

Question Book:
Year 6, pages 2-3

Author / Source:
http://antenna.sciencemuseum.org.uk

Genre:
Non-fiction — interview

Cross-curricular links:

* History (famous inventors)

* Science (technological innovation)

* D&T (testing prototypes)

Introduction

In this interview, computer scientist Floris Ernst describes his work on Nixie, the world's first simple, wearable drone. The interview provides pupils with a first-hand insight into the design and development process behind this cutting-edge technology. Ensure pupils are aware that, in this context, a drone is a small, unmanned aircraft. As they read, pupils should consider what the interview tells them about the process by which scientists and engineers develop new technologies.

Answers

1. E.g. To automatically take photographs of its owner.

2. E.g. Because it is difficult for them to use a camera while they are climbing, so Nixie will allow them to take photos of themselves safely while climbing.

3. E.g. Because they could be used to spy on people and take photos or videos of places that are supposed to be private, for example by flying over people's gardens or looking through windows.

4. E.g. To get a better view of dangerous situations, and to help locate people who need to be rescued.

5. Any appropriate answer. E.g. He is very positive about Nixie, and it seems like he is very passionate about the project — the use of exclamation marks shows this enthusiasm.

6. Any appropriate answer. E.g. Yes, because it would be fun to have a flying camera that could take photos from any angle, especially one like Nixie that would be light and easy to use. OR E.g. No, because it might be used to spy on people. Also, it could be dangerous because it might hurt someone if it crashed.

Extra Activities

* Get pupils to use the information in the interview to design a poster persuading people to buy Nixie. Encourage them to think about how they can use language to make their poster as persuasive as possible.

* Ask pupils to research other inventors and their inventions, such as James Dyson, Trevor Baylis, Mary Anderson, John Logie Baird and Stephanie Kwolek. Pupils should present their findings in the form of an imagined interview with the inventor, using similar questions to those asked in the Nixie interview.

* Using the interview as a starting point, explore the process of technological innovation. Key points to cover include the value of teamwork in developing new technologies; the importance of experimentation in the development process; and the use of prototypes to test and improve design features.

* Working in small groups, challenge pupils to design an aeroplane, made only from A4 sheets of paper, that will fly as far as possible. Once they have designed and built their first prototype, they should test it and use the outcome of the tests to build an improved version of their design. Get pupils to draw a diagram of their final design, annotating the features they added to make it fly further.

Holes

Question Book:
Year 6, pages 4-5

Author / Source:
Louis Sachar

Genre:
Fiction — novel extract

Cross-curricular links:

- Drama (role-play)
- PSHE (juvenile prison)
- Geography (deserts)

Introduction

Louis Sachar's *Holes* tells the unfortunate tale of Stanley Yelnats and his time at Camp Green Lake, a juvenile correctional facility in Texas. Before reading the extract, ask pupils about the novel's title. What might the novel be about? What do they think will happen? As pupils read the text, encourage them to pay special attention to the deliberate use of short sentences, and the impact this has on the reader.

Answers

1. E.g. The lake has dried up, the town has disappeared, and the people who lived in the town have gone.

2. E.g. The narrator is very negative about it. He describes the location as a "wasteland" and makes it sound like an uncomfortable place by emphasising the high temperatures and lack of shade.

3. E.g. A selfish person because she has the only hammock on the site, which is shaded by the only trees, and she won't let the campers use it. She also seems cruel because she makes the campers dig holes all day.

4. E.g. No, because the hot conditions they work in are unbearable, and many are even prepared to risk being bitten by a scorpion or a rattlesnake in order to get a break from digging holes on the lake.

5. Any appropriate answer. E.g. He doesn't really explain why the campers are at Camp Green Lake, so the reader wants to read more to find out how they ended up there.

6. Any appropriate answer. E.g. No, because the conditions the boys have to work in are dangerous and unfair, even if they have done something wrong. OR E.g. Yes, because it might make them change their behaviour in the future so that they wouldn't have to receive the same punishment again.

Extra Activities

- Question 5 asks pupils to consider the techniques Sachar uses to make the reader keep reading. As a class, discuss pupils' answers to this question and explore in more detail the way Sachar engages the reader.

- Ask pupils to write a postcard home as if they were Stanley, writing from Camp Green Lake.

- Divide pupils into pairs and ask them to imagine the first meeting between Stanley and the Warden. They should write a short role-play, which they can then perform for the class.

- The children in *Holes* have been sent away to a correctional facility, or a juvenile prison. With the whole class, discuss various opinions about sending children to prison. How old should a child be before he or she is considered old enough to go to prison? Where should they go if they don't go to prison?

- Camp Green Lake is set in desert-like conditions. Get pupils to look up the word 'desert' in a dictionary, and then assign groups different deserts to investigate (e.g. Antarctica, the Gobi Desert, the Sahara Desert and the Kalahari Desert). Ask pupils to present their findings to the class so that everyone can see the diversity between the different types of desert.

Born on a Blue Day

Question Book:
Year 6, pages 6-7

Author / Source:
Daniel Tammet

Genre:
Non-fiction — memoir

Cross-curricular links:

*   PSHE (autism spectrum)

*   Art (numerical representation)

*   Maths (prime numbers)

Introduction

As well as suffering from Asperger's syndrome, Daniel Tammet has savant syndrome, a rare condition in which individuals with serious mental disorders show remarkable abilities in a specific field, often either art, music, calendar calculation, mathematics or spatial skills. Like Daniel, around fifty per cent of people with savant syndrome suffer from an autism spectrum disorder, although savant syndrome also occurs in individuals with other developmental or neurological disorders. Before you start reading the extract with the class, use the introduction in the Question Book to ensure that pupils have a basic understanding of the nature of Daniel's condition.

Answers

1. E.g. A number that's only divisible by itself and one. Daniel recognises them by their "pebble-like" quality.

2. E.g. He eats exactly 45 grams of porridge for breakfast each morning, weighing the bowl with an electronic scale. Then he counts the number of items of clothing he's wearing before leaving the house. He gets anxious if he can't follow his normal routine.

3. E.g. "Eleven is friendly" and "five is loud".

4. E.g. Because "Times" and "Square" are both words that you might use in maths.

5. E.g. He means that he felt surrounded by enormous things. He links the number nine to "feelings of immensity", so the huge buildings in Times Square made him feel like there were nines all around him.

6. Any appropriate answer. E.g. I think that it would be difficult if you needed to follow the same routine every day, because sometimes things might get in the way of your routine, and that would be very stressful.

Extra Activities

*   *Born on a Blue Day* is a memoir. Memoirs follow similar conventions to autobiographies. With the whole class, discuss the conventions of autobiographical writing. Ask pupils to write a short autobiographical passage, or a memoir, describing how they celebrated their most recent birthday.

*   With the whole class, look at the way Daniel describes the different numbers mentioned in the extract. Ask pupils to suggest how Daniel might see other numbers, and to explain their answers. You could then ask pupils to draw or paint a picture showing the way that Daniel sees some of the numbers he describes in the extract.

*   Ask pupils to write a poem describing how Daniel views his world.

*   With the whole class, discuss the challenges that people living with savant syndrome and other autism spectrum disorders face on a daily basis.

*   Challenge pupils to find all the prime numbers under 100.

2, 3, 5, 7, 11, 13, 17, 19, 23, 29, 31, 37, 41, 43, 47, 53, 59, 61, 67, 71, 73, 79, 83, 89, 97

Hostages to Handheld Devices

Question Book:
Year 6, pages 8-9

Author / Source:
www.independent.co.uk

Genre:
Non-fiction — news article

Cross-curricular links:
- Science (benefits of exercise)
- PE (sport and technology)
- Maths (statistics)

Introduction

Children are spending an increasing amount of time using devices such as mobile phones, tablets and laptops, and this has led to concerns about the health consequences of their increasingly sedentary lifestyles. This article presents recent research into children's attitudes towards technology and sport, raising the possibility of integrating technology into PE lessons in order to increase children's participation in physical activity. Before reading the article with the class, ask pupils whether they prefer playing sports or video games.

Answers

1. E.g. Negative. It says that there are "fears" about the way these devices are affecting children, and the phrase "hostages to handheld devices" makes it sound like children are being taken captive by these devices.

2. "critical crossroads" E.g. Because the alliteration makes the phrase stand out. The phrase also sounds very dramatic because it suggests that major decisions need to be taken about the future of sport in schools.

3. b. enjoy PE lessons

4. E.g. Just because young people enjoy using technology doesn't mean that they aren't interested in other kinds of activities too.

5. a. personification

6. "integrates"

7. E.g. Optimistic. She thinks that primary schools are starting to change the way they look at PE, and she thinks that the number of children doing PE is probably going to go up in the next few years.

Extra Activities

- Get pupils to identify the language and layout features which show that this text is a news article. Can they think of any other features of news articles?

- Get pupils to research the physical and psychological benefits of regular exercise. They should design a leaflet that will persuade primary school children to do more exercise. Encourage them to think about how they can use language and layout to make their leaflet appeal to their target audience.

- With the whole class, discuss the way PE is taught in school. Ask pupils to suggest how modern technology might be incorporated into PE lessons. Do pupils think that integrating PE and technology is a good idea? Would it make them enjoy their PE lessons more?

- Get pupils to carry out a survey of their classmates' participation in sport and other hobbies, asking questions inspired by the text (e.g. "Do you enjoy PE lessons?"), and questions about activities that pupils do in their spare time. Pupils should use bar graphs, pie charts and pictograms to present their results.

Cider With Rosie

Question Book:
Year 6, pages 10-11

Author / Source:
Laurie Lee

Genre:
Autobiographical novel

Cross-curricular links:
*   History (change over time)
*   Geography (the British landscape)

Introduction

Laurie Lee is best known for his autobiographical novel *Cider With Rosie*, first published in 1959. The novel begins just before the end of World War I and follows Lee's experiences growing up in the small Gloucestershire village of Slad. In some respects the novel presents country life as idyllic, but it also explores the hardships of life at that time. By the end of the novel, Slad is beginning to be affected by the changes brought by the post-war years, such as the introduction of the motor car, and people leaving to work in larger towns and cities. This results in the decline of the traditional village life the narrator knew as a child. Make sure pupils read the introduction so that they understand when and where the text is set.

Answers

1.   E.g. Because the grass is unfamiliar and tall, so it seems threatening, and because he is on his own for the first time in his life.

2.   "Snow-clouds of elder-blossom" E.g. It helps you to imagine what the elder-blossom looks like, because it creates a picture of the blossom being white and fluffy, like clouds of snow.

3.   a. c. a simile b. E.g. Comparing the sun to a bully makes it sound cruel and violent. This helps the reader to understand why the narrator feels so frightened and upset.

4.   E.g. Because a shield protects you, and his sisters' faces form a shield that protects him from the sun.

5.   Any appropriate answer. E.g. Yes, because writers often make the natural world sound beautiful, but the narrator makes it sound frightening and horrible. For example, he says that the air smelled "rank".

Extra Activities

*   With the whole class, explore the feelings that Lee conveys in this extract. Ask pupils to suggest one or two adjectives to describe how the narrator feels in each paragraph, and to explain their choices.

*   As a class, identify the language that Lee uses to describe the natural world and explain how it affects the reader. Drawing on their answers to question 5 in the Question Book, get pupils to explain whether they share Lee's view of nature. Ask pupils to rewrite the extract in a way that reflects their own attitude towards the natural world.

*   In small groups, ask pupils to investigate different aspects of life (e.g. education, leisure activities, communication, transport) for children in the early twentieth century. Pupils should share their findings with the class so that they can build up a detailed picture of the similarities and differences between children's lives then and now.

*   The village of Slad is located in the Cotswolds Area of Outstanding Natural Beauty. Give pupils a list of all the AONBs and National Parks in the UK and a map showing their location. Challenge pupils to name the parks on their map and to look for pictures on the Internet of the landscape in some of them.

Olympic Torch Relay, Day 52

Question Book:
Year 6, pages 12-13

Author / Source:
Matt King, www.theguardian.com

Genre:
Non-fiction — news article

Cross-curricular links:
- PSHE (disability and accessibility)
- Geography (world cities)
- History (Ancient Greece)

Introduction

In this article, Matt King, one of the torchbearers for the London 2012 Olympic Torch Relay, describes how he rebuilt his life after a devastating rugby accident left him paralysed from the neck down. Before reading the article with the class, explain that torchbearers like Matt are selected because of their outstanding contribution to their communities and because they are role models to others. As they read, ask pupils to think about why Matt may have been nominated to act as a torchbearer.

Answers

1. E.g. He went back to school to finish his A-levels, went to university, and then got a job at a City law firm.

2. E.g. Because he has suffered a similar injury to them, so he understands what they are going through.

3. E.g. Because some very unusual things have happened, such as receiving an OBE and carrying the Olympic Torch.

4. The day his accident happened. E.g. He calls it a "fateful" day because it was a day that completely changed the course of his life.

5. E.g. He found coaching rugby difficult because it reminded him that he could no longer play rugby himself.

6. Any appropriate answer. E.g. No. Even though he can no longer do some things, such as play rugby, he no longer feels devastated because he has managed to move on and build a successful life for himself.

Extra Activities

- Ask pupils to explain why they think Matt was nominated by his community to act as a torchbearer. Get them to suggest role models in their communities who they would nominate to carry the Olympic torch.

- With the whole class, discuss the physical and social challenges that Matt may have faced when he went back to school after his accident. Ask pupils to identify anything their school has done to make it accessible for pupils with disabilities. What else could the school do to improve accessibility?

- Highlight the use of the first person in this article, and discuss, with the class, its effect on the reader. Discuss other uses of language that add to the impact of the article too.

- Assign groups of pupils different cities around the world, and ask them to prepare a bid for that city to host the next Olympic Games. Their bids might cover the city's size and location, its climate, its existing sports facilities, and how they think the Games would benefit the city and vice versa. Each group should present their bid to the class, and pupils can vote to decide which city should be awarded the Games.

- Get pupils to research the ancient Olympic Games. They should find out when and where the ancient Games began, who took part, and what events were involved. Pupils could use their findings to create a class display showing similarities and differences between the ancient and modern-day Olympic Games.

Poems about Seasons

Question Book:
Year 6, pages 14-15

Author / Source:
Adrian Henri
John Updike

Genre:
Poetry

Cross-curricular links:
• Geography (comparing climates)

Introduction

Adrian Henri was a British poet and painter. One of the influential Liverpool Poets of the 1960s, he is credited with helping to increase the popularity of poetry among young people by writing poems about popular culture. Henri's contemporary, the American writer John Updike, is best known for his novels, but he also published several poetry collections. Like Henri, Updike is known for depicting familiar topics in his poems. This contrasting pair of poems gives pupils the opportunity to compare different forms of poetry, and to explore the use of vivid imagery to describe the world around them.

Answers

1. "The nights come in / early"

2. "there'll be tangerines in the shops, / in shiny paper like Christmas lights"

3. E.g. He means bare trees that are covered in white frost so they look like they're made of lace.

4. E.g. Maybe because the verb "purrs" sounds like the noise that the radiator makes. Also, cats purr when they're happy, so the word "purrs" makes the radiator sound happy.

5. *Autumn*

6. E.g. *Autumn*. It mentions things like fireworks, which are exciting, and it describes enjoyable autumn activities like kicking leaves. *January* describes the cold and dark, which are things most people don't enjoy.

7. Any appropriate answer. E.g. I prefer *January* because I think it describes winter really effectively. For example, the phrase "The sun a spark" helps you imagine how small and distant the sun seems in winter. OR E.g. I prefer *Autumn*, because it mentions lots of my favourite things, like conkers and blackberries. I also like the way it uses different senses, such as smell, to bring the season to life.

Extra Activities

• As a class, compare the form of the two poems. Ask pupils to identify the rhyme scheme and number of syllables per line in *January* and discuss how these features affect the rhythm and tone of the poem. What is different about the form of *Autumn*? How does this affect the poem's rhythm and tone?

• Ask pupils to identify examples of figurative language from the two poems and explain their meaning and effect. Why do they think the poets chose these phrases? Do pupils find them effective?

• Get pupils to write and illustrate their own 16-line poem about their favourite season or month. Their poem should either start "Season of..." and be written in free verse, or follow the same rhyme scheme as *January*.

• *January* was first published while John Updike was living in Massachusetts. Challenge pupils to find Massachusetts on a map and then ask them to research its climate. They should use their findings to write a short text describing what winters are like in Massachusetts and comparing them to winters in the UK. As a class, discuss how Updike's poem might have been different if he had lived in Britain.

A Letter from C.S. Lewis

Question Book:
Year 6, pages 16-17

Author / Source:
C.S. Lewis

Genre:
Non-fiction — letter

Cross-curricular links:
* Art (illustrating a text)

Introduction

Pupils may know C.S. Lewis as the author of *The Chronicles of Narnia*, which are still widely read, and have been adapted for television, radio, stage and film. In this letter, Lewis draws on his many years of experience as an author to offer one of his young fans some helpful advice on how to write well. Before reading the letter with the class, ask pupils to suggest guidelines that they think are important for good writing.

Answers

1. "the setting but not the jewel"

2. E.g. Because he thinks Joan's too young to enjoy it at the moment, and if she reads it now, it will stop her enjoying it when she's older.

3. E.g. He finds it difficult. He says that, as a writer, you very rarely manage to describe "the *thing* itself", even if you write lots of books.

4. d. ambiguity

5. E.g. It tells you that you should use adjectives to make the reader feel a certain way, rather than to tell the reader how they ought to feel.

6. E.g. When writing, writers should avoid ambiguity; use simple language; use concrete nouns rather than abstract ones where possible; and they shouldn't exaggerate or tell the reader how they ought to feel.

Extra Activities

* With the whole class, discuss the advice offered in C.S. Lewis's letter. How does Lewis's advice compare with the guidelines that the pupils suggested before reading the letter? Are pupils surprised by any of Lewis's suggestions? Do they agree or disagree with his advice?

* To highlight the value of simple, direct language, challenge pupils to think of as many ways as possible to describe everyday objects, without using "the plain direct word". For example, a spade might be 'a long-handled excavation device' or 'a manual earth-removal tool'.

* Lewis gives one example where an abstract noun can be replaced with a concrete one ("Mortality rose" / "More people died"). Ask pupils to write sentences containing other abstract nouns, then challenge them to rewrite their sentences, replacing the abstract nouns with concrete ones.

* Ask pupils to write a passage describing a terrifying monster. Following Lewis's advice, they should avoid adjectives like "horrifying", and instead use language to create an image that will terrify the reader.

* Read one of the pupils' passages to the class and ask everyone to draw a picture of the monster it describes. As a class, discuss the similarities and differences between the pupils' drawings. Did the passage create the same image in everyone's mind, or did different pupils imagine it differently?

* Get pupils to write a letter to Lewis, following his advice, to vividly describe their own "Wonderful Night".

The Lord of the Rings

Question Book:
Year 6, pages 18-19

Author / Source:
J.R.R. Tolkien

Genre:
Classic fiction — novel extract

Cross-curricular links:
*   Art (fantasy characters)

Introduction

J.R.R. Tolkien's novel, *The Lord of the Rings*, is extraordinarily popular, and has been a major influence on modern fantasy writing for both children and adults. Tolkien's books are so popular because of the remarkably detailed fantasy world he created, and his use of language to vividly bring this world to life. In this extract, Gandalf (a wizard) and Pippin (a hobbit) are travelling to the great stone city of Minas Tirith. As they read, encourage pupils to think about how Tolkien uses language to create the atmosphere in this extract.

Answers

1. "the wind sang" or "the mountains of the South marched past"

2. E.g. He uses verbs that describe quick movement, such as "was rushing", which show that Gandalf and Pippin are travelling quickly. He also describes the sound of the wind, which emphasises how fast they are moving.

3. E.g. It means that the men were so scared of the "winged shadow" that they shrank away from it.

4. E.g. Because this repetition emphasises how much travelling Gandalf and Pippin have done.

5. E.g. threatening; frightening; sinister

6. E.g. He feels afraid. The verbs "cried" and "clutching" suggest that he is frightened, and the exclamation marks make it seem as if he is shouting in fear.

7. Any appropriate answer. E.g. When Pippin is scared, for example, when the "winged shadow" flies past, Gandalf manages to comfort him. This shows that Pippin trusts Gandalf. However, Pippin is worried about where Gandalf is taking him, so he doesn't trust Gandalf completely.

Extra Activities

*   With the whole class, discuss the techniques that Tolkien uses to create the extract's atmosphere.

*   In this extract, Tolkien uses figurative language to convey the speed of Gandalf and Pippin's journey. Ask pupils to think of their own similes and metaphors that convey a sense of travelling at speed. Pupils should then write a short passage that uses figurative language to describe an imagined journey.

*   Ask pupils to identify features of this extract which show that *The Lord of the Rings* is a work of fantasy. Can they think of any other features that might suggest a book belongs to the fantasy genre? With the whole class, discuss the similarities and differences between fantasy novels and other types of fictional writing.

*   Tolkien's books are filled with a vast array of fantasy characters. Get pupils to imagine their own fantasy character and produce an annotated illustration showing how it looks and behaves. Pupils could share their ideas with the class and write a short story featuring some or all or their classmates' characters.

Queen Victoria's Diary

Question Book:
Year 6, pages 20-21

Author / Source:
Queen Victoria

Genre:
Non-fiction — diary

Cross-curricular links:
• History (sources)

Introduction

Queen Victoria (1819-1901) was the only child of Prince Edward, Duke of Kent, the fourth son of King George III. As her three uncles had no legitimate children, Victoria was heir to the British throne. When the last of her uncles, King William IV, died on 20th June 1837, Victoria became Queen. Throughout her life, Victoria kept a detailed diary, and this extract offers a first-hand account of the day when, aged just 18, she inherited the throne. Before pupils read the diary extract, ensure that they are aware of its historical context. It may be helpful to explain that Victoria knew that King William was seriously ill, and that she would inherit the throne on his death.

Answers

1. E.g. died; passed away

2. E.g. told; informed; notified

3. E.g. Because the Queen wanted him to describe the King's last moments to Victoria.

4. the role of queen

5. E.g. Her "good will" and her desire to do the right thing.

6. E.g. Victoria likes and trusts Lord Melbourne because she thinks that he is "a very straightforward, honest, clever and good man".

7. Any appropriate answer. E.g. She felt sad because her uncle had died. She also felt very calm — her description is very matter-of-fact, and it doesn't suggest strong emotions like surprise or excitement.

Extra Activities

• With the whole class, discuss Victoria's response to the news that she had become queen. Ask pupils to identify the feelings that Victoria puts across in her diary, and to explain whether they find any aspects of her response surprising.

• Ask pupils to imagine how they would feel if, like Victoria, they were woken early in the morning and told that they had become king or queen. Pupils should write a diary entry describing their feelings.

• Some of the language in Queen Victoria's diary seems old-fashioned to the modern reader. Get pupils to work through the extract, updating old-fashioned language with appropriate modern-day equivalents.

• The extract ends "I then wrote a letter to the Queen". With the whole class, discuss what Victoria may have included in this letter, and then ask pupils to write Victoria's letter to the Queen.

• This diary extract is an important primary source for Queen Victoria's accession to the throne. Ask pupils to suggest other sources, both historical and modern, that they could use to find out more about Victoria's accession and coronation. Explain the concept of primary and secondary sources, and ask pupils to categorise the sources they have suggested as either primary or secondary.

If—

Question Book:
Year 6, pages 22-23

Author / Source:
Rudyard Kipling

Genre:
Classic poetry

Cross-curricular links:
*   PSHE (personal development)

Introduction

Rudyard Kipling (1865-1936) is an extremely well-known author, and pupils may previously have come across this poem, or his other works for children, such as *The Jungle Book* or the *Just So Stories*. *If—*, written in 1895 but first published in 1910, remains highly popular, and has repeatedly been voted the nation's favourite poem, even though some of the ideals it presents may seem outdated to a modern audience. Pupils should read the poem closely in order to gain a clear understanding of the ideas that Kipling puts across. Encourage them to form their own opinions about the model of behaviour presented in the poem.

Answers

1. the second person

2. "If you can wait and not be tired by waiting"

3. d. not tell lies

4. b. perseverance

5. E.g. moral behaviour; dignity; honour

6. c. personification

7. Any appropriate answer. E.g. Difficult, because normally you react to them in different ways — you're usually happy about a triumph, and very upset about a disaster.

8. Any appropriate answer. E.g. I think some parts of the poem give good advice, such as the line that says "trust yourself when all men doubt you". However, I don't agree with some of the advice. For example, if things go wrong, I don't think you should keep it a secret like the poem suggests in lines 19-20.

Extra Activities

*   Work through the poem with the whole class, asking pupils to explain the meaning of each statement beginning with "If" in their own words. Encourage pupils to discuss whether they agree or disagree with each point, and to explain the reasons for their opinions.

*   Give pupils a list of abstract nouns and ask them to match each noun to the appropriate part(s) of the poem. → *confidence, patience, honesty, determination...*

*   Kipling wrote *If—* for his son, John. Once pupils have a good understanding of the ideas in the poem, get them to rewrite it in their own words, in the form of a letter from Kipling to his son.

*   With the whole class, discuss the poetic techniques used in the poem, including the ABAB CDCD rhyme scheme and the alternation between lines of 11 and 10 syllables.

*   Ask pupils to identify the qualities they think children should develop while growing up. Get them to write statements beginning with the word 'If' to describe these qualities (e.g. 'If you can keep working at something, even when it's really difficult'), and use their statements to write a poem in the style of *If—*.

Theseus's Adventures

Question Book:
Year 6, pages 24-25

Author / Source:
H.A. Guerber

Genre:
Myth

Cross-curricular links:
- History (Ancient Greece)
- PSHE (democracy)

Introduction

In Greek mythology, Theseus is a great hero, credited with unifying the communities of Attica into the Athenian city-state. It is said that Theseus's father was King Aegeus of Athens. Theseus spent his childhood with his mother, Aethra, in the Peloponnese city of Troezen. When he came of age, Theseus set out for Athens to take his place as heir to his father's kingdom. During his journey, he experienced many adventures, two of which are described in this extract. Before reading the extract with the class, show pupils a map of Greece, highlighting the location of Troezen and Athens. Point out the Isthmus of Corinth, and explain that it is a narrow land bridge linking the Peloponnese peninsula to mainland Greece.

Answers

1. E.g. escaped; avoided; evaded

2. E.g. He used a huge pine tree to throw Sinis into the air so that he would smash into the mountain side.

3. E.g. Because the Isthmus was very narrow, and Sciron guarded the only possible path.

4. to devour

5. E.g. He felt afraid. He had killed all the people who had washed his feet, so he was afraid that Theseus was going to kill him in the same way.

6. E.g. It includes a giant. OR E.g. It includes a huge, man-eating tortoise. OR E.g. It includes a hero who must complete some difficult tasks.

7. Any appropriate answer. E.g. Yes, because he easily managed to defeat Sinis and Sciron, so I think he would also have been able to survive any other dangers that he might have faced on the way to Athens.

Extra Activities

- Get pupils to identify all the adjectives in this extract. Working in small groups, they should try to think of as many synonyms as possible for each adjective.

- Ask pupils to write a news article reporting the adventures described in this extract. Encourage them to use appropriate language and presentational features.

- Ask pupils to imagine what adventure Theseus might have experienced next on his journey to Athens. They should write a continuation of this extract, describing what they think happened next.

- Question 6 in the Question Book asks about the conventions of myths. As a class, discuss pupils' answers to this question. Can pupils think of any other conventions that might mark a text out as a myth?

- Athens is widely regarded as the birth-place of democracy. Ask pupils to research Athenian democracy, focusing on who was and was not allowed to participate, the make-up and role of the assembly and the courts, and the methods by which officeholders were selected. Pupils should use their findings to create a poster explaining the key features of Athenian democracy.

I Can Jump Puddles

Question Book:
Year 6, pages 26-27

Author / Source:
Alan Marshall

Genre:
Non-fiction — autobiography

Cross-curricular links:
*   PSHE (disability)
*   Geography (Australia; tourism)

Introduction

Polio (Infantile Paralysis) is an infectious disease which became widespread in Europe, north America and Australasia in the first half of the twentieth century. Although it has now been largely eradicated in these regions, polio remains endemic in parts of Africa and south Asia. While most of those who contract polio experience no symptoms, in some cases, the disease can result in muscle weakness, paralysis or even death. In this extract, the Australian writer Alan Marshall (1902-1984), who contracted polio at the age of six, describes how his small, rural hometown reacted to his illness. Make sure pupils read the introduction so they understand that the illness Alan describes had a lasting physical impact upon him.

Answers

1. E.g. question

2. a. d. curiosity b. E.g. They ask questions about him, and they look at his house "with a new interest". This shows that they are curious about his illness.

3. E.g. Because they were worried their children would catch polio too, and they thought that they might be able to prevent them from getting ill by wrapping them up warmly.

4. "It hits you like a blow from God"

5. E.g. I think he felt pessimistic. He says "that was the end of him", which suggests that he didn't think Alan was going to recover.

6. E.g. It suggests that he didn't let his disability stop him doing the things he wanted to do. Even though the illness meant that it was difficult for him to walk, he still found a way to jump puddles.

Extra Activities

*   Drawing on their answers to question 6 in the Question Book, ask pupils to write a letter from the young Alan to a friend, describing how having polio has affected him and how he feels about the disease.

*   With the whole class, identify the features of the extract that show it's an example of autobiographical writing. How would the extract be different if it were a biography? As a class, make a list of similarities and differences between biographies and autobiographies.

*   Get pupils to write an autobiographical passage describing a vivid memory from when they were younger.

*   Ask pupils to research their favourite author and write a brief biography about them.

*   Explain to pupils that, despite his disability, Alan Marshall went on to have a very successful writing career. Ask pupils to create posters celebrating the achievements of other individuals who have overcome adversity, such as Franklin D. Roosevelt, Stephen Hawking, Helen Keller and Tanni Grey-Thompson.

*   Alan Marshall grew up in the Australian state of Victoria. Ask pupils to find out where Victoria is and to research its climate, geographical features, major cities and tourist attractions. They should use their findings to create a page for a tourism website that will persuade people to visit Victoria.

White Fang

Question Book:
Year 6, pages 28-29

Author / Source:
Jack London

Genre:
Classic fiction — novel extract

Cross-curricular links:
- Geography (Yukon Territory)
- Science (adaptation and evolution)

Introduction

Jack London is a popular author, and many pupils may have previously come across this novel, or some of his others, such as *Call of the Wild*. Ensure pupils read the introduction to the extract so that they understand who White Fang is, and then focus their attention on London's vivid use of language.

Answers

1. E.g. That the tribe was leaving, and he would have to go with them.

2. E.g. He feels afraid. Maybe he is frightened that Grey Beaver will punish him if he finds him.

3. E.g. sinister; menacing; forbidding; threatening

4. E.g. White Fang feels frightened of being alone in the woods. The author shows this by using adjectives like "looming" and "perilous" to make the setting seem frightening. He also describes White Fang with words like "perturbed" and "suspicious", which show that he feels anxious and frightened.

5. E.g. It suggests that the cold is so intense that it has got inside White Fang's body. This shows the reader how cold it is, and helps them to imagine how it felt.

6. E.g. The fact that he had run away suggests that he may not have liked living in the camp very much, so he didn't want to return, even when he was cold and hungry. He may also have stayed away because he wanted to be independent or because he didn't know where the camp had moved to.

Extra Activities

- With the whole class, discuss how Jack London uses language to convey a sense of place within this extract (e.g. the use of language to convey the cold of a Canadian autumn; the use of adjectives to make the woods seem frightening). Suggest some alternative settings (e.g. a busy city street; a beach during a storm) and ask pupils to think of similarly evocative words and phrases to describe them.

- Ask pupils to imagine finding themselves alone in an unfamiliar environment. Get them to write a short passage describing the atmosphere and their feelings about being alone.

- In this passage, Jack London describes White Fang's "memory-pictures" of the camp. Ask pupils to write and illustrate a paragraph describing their "memory-pictures" of a place that is familiar to them.

- This extract is written from White Fang's perspective. Get pupils to choose their favourite animal and write a short story from that animal's perspective. Encourage them to think about the ways in which their chosen animal might see the world differently than humans do.

- This extract is set in the Yukon Territory in north-western Canada. Ask groups of pupils to research different aspects of the Yukon's climate and geography and present their findings to the class.

- Show pupils pictures of wild animals (e.g. wolves, camels, polar bears) and their habitats. Ask pupils to match each animal to its habitat and discuss the physical features that enable it to survive there. Explain how, over time, variation in offspring can make animals more or less suited to particular environments.

Macbeth

Question Book:
Year 6, pages 30-31

Author / Source:
William Shakespeare

Genre:
Classic fiction — playscript

Cross-curricular links:
- Drama (performance)
- Art (cartoon strip)
- PSHE (ambition)

Introduction

Born in 1564, William Shakespeare is widely regarded as one of the greatest writers in the English language. *Macbeth*, one of his darkest and most powerful tragedies, is about the corrupting power of ambition. In this key scene from the first act, Macbeth and Banquo encounter The Three Witches, who deliver the fateful prophecy that one day Macbeth will be king. This may be pupils' first experience of reading Shakespeare, and they will almost certainly find some of the language challenging. Before pupils read the extract, explain that in Shakespearian English, the word order is sometimes different than in modern English, and that apostrophes are sometimes used to represent missing letters. Encourage pupils to use the punctuation to guide them through the text, rather than stopping at the end of each line.

Answers

1. not like the inhabitants of the earth (1 mark for two correct; 2 marks for all correct)

2. E.g. They are wrinkled and are wearing such strange clothes that they look as if they could have come from a different planet. They have thin lips and beards.

3. E.g. Because they seem like women, but they have beards, which are normally associated with men.

4. E.g. It shows that Macbeth is shocked by the prophecy ("you start"), and that he seems afraid.

5. "Are ye fantastical"

6. c. a metaphor

7. E.g. No, he doesn't seem frightened of The Witches. He thinks that the things they tell Macbeth sound positive, not frightening. He also says that he isn't afraid of The Witches hating him.

Extra Activities

- Ask pupils to summarise the extract. Then work through the extract with the whole class, explaining any unfamiliar vocabulary and discussing the meaning of each sentence. Encourage pupils to explain each line in their own words.

- Divide the class into small groups and ask them to rewrite the extract using modern language, punctuation and grammar. Pupils should then perform their modernised versions for the class.

- Get pupils to transform the extract into a cartoon strip. Encourage them to try to convey the way The Witches look, and the contrasting ways in which Macbeth and Banquo respond to The Witches' prophecy.

- As a class, discuss ambition. Explain that The Witches' prophecy described in the extract leads to Macbeth being corrupted and ultimately destroyed by his ambition for power. Ask pupils to explain their opinions about ambition. What are their ambitions? Do they think ambition is something positive or negative? Are they surprised by the negative image of ambition that Macbeth represents?

Pupil Progress Chart — Year 3

Average score out of 10																												
Carrie's War																												
Jellyfish in the UK																												
The Secret History of Tom Trueheart																												
Poems about Crocodiles																												
My Name is Mina																												
An Interview with Rebecca Adlington																												
High Adventure																												
Robotic Baby Penguin																												
The Demon Headmaster																												
Daddy Fell into the Pond																												
Let's Get Growing!																												
Bill's New Frock																												
Nature Trail																												
Building Stonehenge																												
Harriet's Hare																												
Class .... Pupil Name																												

▢ = non-fiction   ▨ = fiction

Pupil Progress Chart — Year 4

Average score out of 10																										
Swim, Bike, Run: Our Triathlon Story																										
Poems about Witches																										
Bletchley Park Codebreakers																										
Peter Pan																										
Reign of the Sea Dragons																										
The Girl Who Walked On Air																										
Chinese New Year																										
The Real Princess																										
BBC Women's Footballer of the Year																										
Hamish and the Worldstoppers																										
Harry Drinkwater's Diary																										
An Interview with Jacqueline Wilson																										
Aesop's Fables																										
The Tale of Custard the Dragon																										
Choosing a Bike																										
Class .... Pupil Name																										

☐ = non-fiction   ▨ = fiction

Pupil Progress Chart — Year 5

Average score out of 10																					
The Wolves of Willoughby Chase																					
Wolves in the UK																					
Hiding Out																					
The Wind in the Willows (musical)																					
Poems about Knights																					
A Letter from E.B. White																					
Tracking Basking Sharks																					
From a Railway Carriage																					
Pompeii																					
The Iron Man																					
The Great Fire of London																					
Tales of King Arthur																					
Why Recycle?																					
An Astronaut's Guide to Life on Earth																					
The Word Party																					
Class .... **Pupil Name**																					

ECT21

☐ = non-fiction (incl. *The Great Fire of London* — poem based on real events)   ▦ = fiction